Praise for Karen Casey

"Karen Casey captures the experience, strength, and hope that are essential to maintaining healthy relationships with each other and with ourselves."
—William C. Moyers, author of *Broken*

"You just can't go wrong with Karen Casey."
—Earnie Larsen, author of *Stage II Recovery* and *From Anger to Forgiveness*

"Karen Casey's honesty about detachment as a lifelong process brings comfort and encouragement. Thanks, Karen, for writing this book and for a lifetime of dedicated service that has made this world a better place."
—Melody Beattie, author of *Codependent No More*

"Veteran self-help author Casey's gentle advice is anchored in a strong spiritual commitment. . . . [She] recommends quieting the mind by letting go of your ego and looking for the lesson in every experience and encounter, whether positive or negative. Casey's voice is thoughtful and accessible."
—*Publishers Weekly*

"*Codependence and the Power of Detachment* should be required reading for all who seek to create healthy, balanced relationships in their lives."
—Claudia Black, PhD, author of *It Will Never Happen to Me*

"*Codependence and the Power of Detachment* is a remarkable book written in easy-to-understand language with great honesty."
—Jerry Jampolsky, MD, founder of the International Center for Attitudinal Healing

"*All We Have Is All We Need* is a gem of a book! So much wisdom and peace in every paragraph and sentence. These inspirational, quotable thoughts constantly affirm the incredible fruits of simply shifting our perspective—through the uniquely human gift of choice."
—Stephen R. Covey, author of *The 7 Habits of Highly Effective People*

getting unstuck

a workbook based on the principles in

Change Your Mind and Your Life Will Follow

KAREN CASEY, PHD

Conari Press

First published in 2012 by Conari Press, an imprint of
Red Wheel/Weiser, LLC
With offices at:
665 Third Street, Suite 400
San Francisco, CA 94107

ISBN: 978-1-57324-548-7

Cover design by Jim Warner
Cover photograph © Exactostock/SuperStock
Interior design by Jane Hagaman
Typeset in Sabon

Printed in the United States of America

I want to dedicate this book to all of you who have been loyal readers and supporters since my first book was published in 1982. I certainly had no expectation then that *Each Day a New Beginning* was charting a new direction for my life.

It's been a surprising journey, a sacred journey, and one that has steeped me in hope for the rest of my life, too.

The men and women who have traveled with me have sustained me in ways that I could never have fathomed.

And then there is my husband, Joe. He is the best in every way. He makes me laugh; he solves my computer problems; he accepts my defects, knowing that I am not perfect but I am always improving. He loves me just as I am, the same way I love him.

Blessings on all of you.

contents

acknowledgments

There are so many people to acknowledge that I don't know where to begin. But first, I must thank Jan Johnson for being present in my world for so many decades. She has been a supporter, a colleague, my publisher, and a good friend.

I want to acknowledge the significant women and men in my life, too. They have shown me the "way to go." All the wisdom I have gathered over the years has come from their many voices. I am so glad I have been a good listener. Blessings on all of you.

introduction

I am so glad you have selected this book to read. It's a book about change, a book that will help you make the kind of changes that are necessary if you want to enjoy a life that's peaceful. It's a book that will keep the process for making the changes simple, doable, and at the end of the day, successful. I can promise you that.

It's the third book in the Change Your Mind and Your Life Will Follow series. In this workbook, I lead you very carefully through key ideas from the original book in case you haven't read it. Worry not; you will be brought up to speed. And if you did already read *Change Your Mind and your Life Will Follow* and its companion, *It's Up to You*, you might discover that this one is the most helpful of all. I say that because it leads you gently through the many ideas from the first book while directing you, in a detailed way, to dig into your own patterns of behavior and write about those areas that keep you stuck, discerning what caused the "stuckness" and developing strategies for getting unstuck.

Being stuck is common to caring people, and indeed, those of us who are trying to grow and change are, more often than not, caring people. Helping each other get unstuck is the next important agenda item. I see that as one of my "assignments" on this journey we are sharing.

The intent of this book, then, is not to eliminate the gift we have for caring about others but to help us see where we should draw boundaries between ourselves and the many others who are intentionally traveling this path with us. It's very easy to turn caring into control, and we must strive to avoid that. Therefore, this book specifically addresses how to care about but not control others. It helps you discover how to discern what is your business and what is not your business. It guides you to let your loved ones find their own Higher Power, teaching you, in the process, how to strengthen your relationship with yours. Accepting that outcomes are God's purview is another tool that this book highlights. Powerlessness, and the power of embracing this in our lives, is a key component of this book as well. And there are many more.

You receive good, orderly direction as we proceed. You can change. You can change any behavior that is hindering your peace of mind. I can promise you this based on personal experience. Gratefully, I have been a practitioner of these principles for change for many years now. Peace is the by-product of living this way, and healthy, interdependent partners in the home, on the job, and in the wider circle of friendships know that these principles work. Now you can join their ranks.

We are beginning an exciting undertaking here. There is no timeline for completion, but I think that once you have begun, you will want to keep moving forward. Change is exhilarating though formidable at times. With the help of this book, you do not attempt huge changes all at once. We will slowly, deliberately, and very carefully move together through the suggested areas for exploration. In the process, we discover who we really are and what changes we should make so we can grow into the people we'd rather be.

In the chapters that follow, there are writing exercises that I have divided into separate questions and journaling prompts. It's not necessary to write every day, but some will see the wisdom of that. Take one question a day if that makes it more manageable, or spend a whole week. But this is only a suggestion, so don't let my proposed pace deter your enthusiasm for forward movement if you'd like to move through the workbook faster. This is your book, your growth. I'm simply the teacher guiding your process. You are the student who will determine your readiness and your pace.

To help you get started each and every day, meditate a few moments first. Perhaps it will help to ask the God of your understanding to walk with you on this part of your journey. Then, and only then, begin to write.

And remember, this is your journal. It's only for others if you want to share it.

Take all the time and space you need. Use an extra journal if you run out of room in the spaces provided or if you find an idea that resonates very deeply with you. Some of you may even want to create a "picture board" that reflects the changes you hope to experience as you progress in this process of growth.

Remember, time is not of the essence. The point of this is for you to gain some objectivity on your interactions, thoughts, and behaviors. The speed of change is not the focus. Throughout this investigation and rumination process, be honest, be specific, and be thorough. Thoroughness leads to growth and change, and is absolutely necessary if we really want to change our state of mind and the tenor of our relationships.

Have fun, however, as you proceed. That's the real gift of a book such as this. It will be like watching a seedling becoming an ear of corn or a butterfly emerging from a cocoon. Your changes will probably be noted by others before you can see them yourself. That's normal. And you will feel blessed by the ease with which you will learn to live "in" the changes. It's about the attainment of peace, after all. That's the purpose I am intent on clarifying for you. That's now become my life's purpose, in fact.

Ready? Let's begin.

let go

**Tending your own garden
is a soul-searching commitment.**

I have found that it's very easy to deny how "attached" we are to the presence of the others who are journeying with us. It's surely never wrong to be attentive to the presence of the many others around us. In fact, being attentive, witnessing the lives of others, is the highest compliment we can pay them, and one we should make. But letting anyone else take center stage in the drama of our life is the very thing that prevents us from actually living our own life. Letting any one of the many others journeying with us have the central role on our stage means we live in the wings of their life. Remaining central on our own stage is the goal of a life well lived.

Accepting that other people are instrumental to our growth and our personal discoveries as well as our joy is far different from dancing around them and thinking that's the purpose for which we, and they, were born. But if dancing too close to others has been your primary focus in life up until now, get ready for a great ride. There is another way to live, and with the help of this book and the guidelines it offers, you are about to begin the practice of that new way. I think you will be thrilled by the changes in perception you will begin to experience. Remember, it's not about leaving any particular person behind, or any relationship behind. Rather, it's about daily discovering and then maintaining the right balance of anyone else's presence.

Changing Old Behaviors

The cultivation of new behaviors can only make sense if we have a clear picture of our old behaviors. So that's where we must begin. We will look closely at ourselves to see and appreciate all of whom we currently are. Just because we are intent on making changes doesn't mean we should disgustedly discard the person we were before we committed to change. We can only be where we are. Where we go next is the purpose of this undertaking. As the saying goes, "Wherever we go, there we are," but we "are" who we want to be in the next moment if we are intent on becoming the corn or the butterfly rather than remaining the seedling or the cocoon.

I want to reiterate, the intent of this workbook is not to make us feel ashamed about who we were last year or even yesterday. We were the best we could be at that time. But that was then. We are in a new space, a new moment, now. This book drew your attention, so the time is right to make some changes in how you think and act.

Let's begin our investigation.

Look at Your Old Behaviors

Who do you think you need to "watch over" right now? Your spouse? Your son or daughter? Maybe a good friend who has always clung to you? And why?

What do you think would happen if you walked away from those people and gave up your suggestions about how they might live (which, to be honest, is a subterfuge anyway)?

Expecting them to do your will—in other words, do exactly as you have planned—is actually your agenda, isn't it? What would happen if you let them sort out their own plans or goals, or solve their own challenges?

Are you afraid they would be lost to you if you turned them loose? How would that look?

Are you concerned that without your attention to their life, they'd discover they don't need you?

Are you afraid they would seek a new "caretaker"?

What are your most common behaviors with them?

Do you make unwanted or unnecessary suggestions?

Do you try to subtly manipulate what they might be thinking or planning to do?

How do you feel when confronted about your actions?

Fostering New Behaviors

Envision how your life could or would look if you paid more attention to it, rather than to the life of someone else. Might you change careers, go back to school, downsize your home, pick up a hobby that you have always secretly longed to do but for which you felt you had too little time? Dream big. Be daring with your thoughts. Dreaming doesn't commit you to fulfilling the desired change yet, but it is the hook that can pull you into forward motion.

I have a friend who decided to take up ballroom dancing a few years ago. Her spouse wasn't interested, but she decided to live out her dream anyway. Her shifting her focus to her own life actually improved their marriage. Another friend joined a fiction-writing group. She doubts she will ever publish one of her short stories, but she has gone on to take many classes and loves the connections she has made with the men and women who, like her, write for the love of it and then read to one another in weekly groups. It has given her life a structure that had been missing ever since she became an empty-nester. A third friend, a former flight attendant, decided to volunteer in the schools to work with children who were failing in reading. In the process, she discovered a new talent. She could motivate children to learn, so she organized an after-school reading program that has been a great success. I took a watercolor class two years ago and now have three of my paintings hanging in my kitchen.

What we envision can take many forms. There isn't a right one or a wrong one. It can be a solitary pursuit or one that includes others. But if you know in your heart you need to move your focus off of someone else's life, having no vision is the glue that holds you in a waiting pattern. We can't become what we can't clearly see in our mind's eye. Don't be embarrassed by your dreams. They are God given, I believe. I think God can read our hearts even when we don't voice our thoughts. He is ushering to our minds what we have yet to say out loud.

Begin Your Plan for Change

Close your eyes if it helps, go to that favorite place in your mind, and see yourself at play, or maybe in a play, or working in a new job, or sitting in a classroom. Don't let my suggestions limit you in any way. Let your desires drive your dream.

Dream in the space below. It's not for public consumption but your own edification. Be as specific as possible.

I can see myself . . . And it would look like . . . And I would feel . . .

Staying Out of the Center of Someone Else's Life

Being central to the lives of others has been our self-proclaimed job for far too long. As I pointed out in detail in *Change Your Mind and Your Life Will Follow* and again in *It's Up To You*, being a partner is one thing, but being the main cog in the center of someone else's wheel, or vice versa, is not why we have partnered up. We have joined the lives of others because of the shared experiences we are meant to have, experiences that were decided on even before we actually met one another here in this realm of worldly existence.

The life experiences we selected before arriving here have allowed us to make the very contributions that were intended for us and those who walk with us. Because we more than likely forgot those selections we made (at least according to Caroline Myss, a spiritual intuitive) and their concomitant choices in this worldly realm, resistance to what drew our attention hindered us on many occasions. But the inkling to make the choice lingered until we finally surrendered to it. That's the fortunate aspect to this journey. Our lessons linger within our choices until we succumb to them. They will wait patiently until they get our attention. They won't shame us or haunt us. They will make no demands. They will simply wait in the wings until we are ready for them.

For many of us, one of the selected primary lessons was to give up hostage taking. Simply put, this is minding someone else's business so that they will have no business that is separate from us. Making this our focus means we never have to experience life alone, or so we think. Nor do we want those individuals to live a life separate from us. The irony is that those people we take as hostages will find a way to leave us eventually. This is a certainty. And it's then that the real lesson is learned. We are alive for the purpose of walking *with* one another, not *for* one another.

Hostage Taking

Because this is such an important area for most of us, let's carefully inventory our past relationships. Let's look at them in great detail, going back to childhood, if necessary. My own clinging had its roots there. The same might be true for you. Let my words prepare you for this part of the journey into your past.

This is a very important exercise. Don't cheat yourself of the growth it will allow you. You are the one seeking growth and peace, both of which are guaranteed if you do your work. What's important is to recognize the similarities in the hostages you felt compelled to take and the feelings that drove you to this obsession with them.

Read through the questions below and meditate on them before answering. Ask the Holy Spirit to be with you as you look into the window of your past. After you have had a chance to open your heart to the Holy Spirit within, write for a while about the hostages you have taken over the years, those you still hang on to, and those you have released or are ready to release. Give this plenty of time. Take each question that is posed below separately. Delve deep. Include all that you can think of from childhood on.

Envision your earliest friends. How did you relate to them?

Were you filled with gladness or fear? Give some instances. What prompted the fear, if that was paramount?

To whom did you turn for comfort or support for your feelings? How did that look?

As you progressed in years, did your behavior change? If so, in what way, specifically? Did you cling? Do you still cling? To whom? How did or do you feel about this? Did fear rule your feelings? What still needs to change?

Are you content with your primary relationships now? If one or more of them still mimics some of those in the past, in what ways?

Can you envision your primary relationships as peaceful? How would they look? How would you feel about them? About the rest of your life? Be specific with an instance that you'd like to change.

Write a paragraph describing to a potential sponsee, or simply a friend who is troubled, what you have learned about the emotional repercussions of hostage taking.

Affirmations can be helpful if you find yourself back in this situation again. Here is an example:

**I remember that my companions
walk beside me, not behind me or in front of me.
They have been sent by God.**

Now write three affirmations that meet your needs. The affirmations can be as simple as a slogan.

Affirmation 1:

Affirmation 2:

Affirmation 3:

Consider this exercise of paramount importance. Repeat these affirmations to yourself in the early morning and throughout the day, any time you are filled with doubt about where to place your focus. Let them permeate your soul. I have found that carrying affirmations in a pocket is helpful. They stay close to my recall then.

Life without Hostages

What does life without hostages look like? For many of us, such a life seems unfathomable, initially. Our whole reason for living, we thought, was to be in charge of someone else's life. *A Life of My Own*, a book I wrote a number of years ago, contains 366 daily meditations about this very topic. I wrote that book as a way of trying to help myself, of course—the reason any author writes any self-help book, I think. I'd like to include one here as an example of the point I'm trying to make:

Live and let live is good advice.

The more comfortable we are with the knowledge that each of us has a unique journey to make, a specific purpose to fulfill, the easier it is to let other people live their own lives. When family members are in trouble with alcohol or other drugs, it's terribly difficult to let them have their own journey. Because we love them, we feel compelled to help them get clean and sober. In reality, all we can do is pray for their safety and well-being. Their recovery is up to them and their Higher Power.

For some of us, it's a leap of faith to believe there really is a Divine plan of which we are a part. And perhaps it's not even necessary to believe. But we'll find the hours of every day gentler if we accept that a Higher Power is watching over all of us.

Being able to let others live and learn their own lessons is one of our lessons. The more we master it, the more peaceful we'll be.

Daily Meditation

A daily meditation that focuses on acceptance of others might help your day go in the right, more peaceful direction.

Take a few minutes to respond, in writing, to the following meditation. How does it call to you? If it's helpful, explain how. Are there soothing aspects to it?

**I have enough to do just living my own life today.
I can let others do what they must.**

Write a mediation that's specifically for yourself. If there are particular people you are trying to let go, name them. And seek the help of your Higher Power. Use the following title to help you focus your attention.

Letting go is my opportunity now.

getting unstuck

**Being focused on the problem prevents us
from being open to the solution, making it unavailable
to us, but we can learn how to refocus.**

This is the work of chapter 2: learning how to open our eyes and our hearts to a new way of seeing and feeling. It's not difficult work, but it is intense in the sense that it takes more than just a little willingness to want to see the solution rather than wallow in the problem. Wallowing in problems is how many live for most of their lives. In fact, we all know some people who never choose to live any other way. And there's a good reason for that. Being open to a solution makes it hard to avoid taking the next step, which is to execute it. Execution means change. For many, change of any kind, be it large or tiny, is formidable.

We all know individuals, and maybe used to be those individuals, who whined about a problem incessantly. Never being open to suggestions for seeing a situation differently is a common defect. The "Yeah but" syndrome, it's called. I well remember in the early years of my recovery calling my friend Rita with the same poor-me complaint, nearly every day. More than once a day even. And finally she had had enough. I had not seriously considered any of her previous and frequent suggestions. "So what," she disgustedly said one day. Stunned, I hung up, both hurt and miffed. Little did I know in that moment what a favor she had done me. I was stuck, and her dismissal of my stuckness helped me see what a whiner I was. It also helped me consider that just maybe there was a different way to live.

I thanked her many times over the subsequent years of our friendship. That lesson showed me two things: the value of a friend who will be straight with you and the importance of finally giving up an old paradigm. We live too easily in the grips of old paradigms, but until we are willing to consider that there is another perspective, we simply don't move on. We don't grow. We don't become who we have been sent here to be.

My paradigm was that I'd always be abandoned. I had felt it with my childhood girlfriends, my first significant boyfriend, my first husband, and every man after him and before my present husband. I am happy to say that fear no longer holds me hostage, but I was in its grips for decades. Naming it and learning what had given rise to it gradually released me from it. I want to share the story of how my release was triggered, as it might help trigger a similar release in you. What this workbook is about, after all, is changing how we see ourselves so we can develop into the man or woman we are "scheduled" to become.

My fear of abandonment was crippling, at times. I watched others like a hawk to see if I could discern their thoughts about me. Did they like me? Did they want me as a best friend? In the sixth grade, when my best friend, Marcia, became best friends with the new girl at our school, Mary, I was devastated. What about her loyalty to me? Day after day, I raced home from school to get my bike to ride as fast as I could to Marcia's before she had a chance to ride off someplace with Mary. And day after day, they had already gone before I got there.

I can still vividly remember crying to my mother, whose response was anything but understanding. It wasn't even particularly gentle. I think my pain might have been too close to her own pain for her to easily comfort me.

This scenario played out repeatedly in other relationships, not in specific content but in form. I felt as if I was on the outside looking in and others were oblivious to my presence. In desperation, I finally spoke to a therapist while in early recovery, and she said she sensed I had been abandoned in the womb. I was mystified, but intrigued, by her words. It was her belief that this was at the root of my unyielding insecurity, particularly around men.

It was in that next year that I had the opportunity to speak to my mother about her life, how she felt about it, what pleased her or disappointed her. And much to my amazement, she began to sob. I had seen her tears on many occasions, but they were nothing like this. Her sobs shook her body. She had never felt like a good mother, she said. She had never thought she was a good wife, either. And the bomb she dropped next was that she had never wanted to give birth to me. Indeed, I had been abandoned in the womb. And she felt so sad and ashamed and was certain it had caused my alcoholism. She had carried this feeling of shame for nearly four decades, never revealing her feelings to anyone.

We held each other, and I was able to assure her she wasn't to blame for my alcoholism, and in that moment, I was profoundly relieved. Her honesty gave me real peace of mind. I can't say that lingering fears of abandonment didn't surface for a time, but they slowly ebbed. In time, they were completely gone, never to return. I could have kept them alive though.

That's the insidiousness of not being willing to let a problem go when there is new information. As we have heard repeatedly, within every problem lies the solution. Within my fear of abandonment was the missing information I needed from my mother, and it was that information that changed my picture. I could have been angry at her for having those feelings about her pregnancy with me. I could have blamed her for all the anguish I had felt for so many years. Or I could make another choice about the entire situation. Making that other choice began the real healing that was so necessary for both of us. And my gratitude for my willingness to choose once again has been a great lesson.

We so easily get stuck in feelings that aren't fruitful, forgetting that they are not facts, or obsessing about situations that are over, playing again and again the same tapes about "him" or "her" or "them." And the reality of most of the tapes is that they detail situations that were generally quite ordinary and deserving of a "so what!" more often than not. And if they weren't ordinary, they are still past, history, and need not become part of the present circumstance. The question to ask whenever we feel trapped in our mind is, Am I helping myself with this thought? If the answer is no, which it will commonly be, let it go.

Obsessions

Let's begin this exercise with a time of quiet meditation. Take a deep breath. Relax your shoulders and your arms and your torso. Breathe deeply and quietly for a few minutes, clearing your mind of today. When you feel quiet within, read on.

Let's revisit some of the feelings that have kept you from moving forward in your life. Abandonment was my big one, as I illustrated above. Was there a really big one for you? Some past situations or imagined slights may still trouble us. We love to obsess. However, we can let them go. Now. They want to be freed from our grip, in fact.

Now take time to respond to each of the following queries with as much detail as you can. Focus on one or two a day preferably. It's not about getting done but about making progress on your personal growth curve.

What do you find yourself focusing on when experiencing downtime?

Is some past situation or assumption still troubling you today when you have work you need to get done?

Did it develop in your childhood? Or as a young adult? Does it matter which?

Did your family of origin contribute to these feelings that still cause you distress, or was it limited to friendships? Have you ever wondered why it was one or the other?

When was this feeling triggered for the first time? What were the circumstances? This is a very important one to explore.

In what realm or circumstance of your life has this obsession hindered you the most? (This is a key idea. Be honest. Be thorough.)

Are there signs of growth, of letting go of unhelpful thoughts or feelings, that you can point to now? (This one will be particularly fun to write about. Enjoy this. The following question is related. Perhaps you can do both in this sitting.)

How has the process of letting these go manifested in your current circumstances?

Can you envision applying the principle of letting go to any remaining obsessive thoughts or feelings? How would your new behavior look? (This is the real crux of the exploration here. Be thorough.)

What's the one (or more) feeling that still gets too much rent-free space in your mind? What's the most troubling aspect of this remaining feeling? (This is the most niggling issue of all. Dig deep!)

The Past Has Much to Teach Us, as Long as We Don't Dwell There

Here is another story that I want to share because it has influenced the rest of my life in a profound way. I want you to watch for similar occurrences in your life. It is an illustration of how letting past, generally erroneous assumptions, define present (or current) circumstances.

I had tried for weeks to get the last professor on my PhD committee to meet with me about my dissertation. He was always unavailable. I sensed he simply had not read it yet. But I was also terrified that he was going to label it as unworthy, which felt like a fate worse than death at that time. When he finally agreed to see me, I sat across from him, and his first words, without even looking directly at me, were "This has to be completely rewritten."

I was stunned. And angry. And afraid. My worst fears were materializing.

I took a very deep breath and asked him if he would agree to go through it with me. Surprisingly, he said yes. For three and a half hours we talked. He posed questions, and I, totally unaware of my words, supplied answers. It felt like an out-of-body experience. I watched him and me but felt removed from it all.

At the end of the exchange, he looked up, smiled for the first time, signed his name across the form, and said, "I'm satisfied. See you at the oral."

I walked out as stunned as when he had first spoken. What I knew to be true, however, was that I had surrendered, and just as I had been promised, God showed up.

This experience changed me in a profound way. I finally understood what was meant by our needing to get out of God's way so that He can work out the details of whatever circumstance has confronted us. I finally understood what was meant about not living in the fear and the baggage of the past. I finally understood that God would do for me what I felt unable to do for myself.

I could have overreacted to my professor in that moment, and that would have been a more common choice for me, but pausing a moment and taking a breath changed the experience, and my life, too. Because of this experience, I have successfully refrained from overreacting to many situations, regardless of their gravity. I have learned that God is in the details. I have learned that God can be trusted to take over. And I have learned that the experience, itself, is the trigger for the next level of growth for which I have been made ready.

Nothing I have shared is unique to me. Perhaps the specific content doesn't match your experiences, but the form is always the same.

Take a look now at your own journey, at the downside of those times you overreacted or the lessons you learned when you did not. All of it is worth savoring. This is your life, after all. And our journey together is designed to make the changes that will promise us greater peace.

Overreacting

Let's meditate for a few moments to prepare our minds for these writing exercises.

Take a deep breath. Take another one. Close your eyes now for a minute or two, and invite God into your present moment.

When you feel ready to begin, open your eyes. Let's look closely at ourselves once again.

Where do you see evidence of overreacting in your life? If this question fits for you, write about it. If it doesn't describe you any longer, how did you get free of the behavior?

Where is there evidence of measurable growth? This question is tied to the one that follows. You might want to answer both of them together.

What was/is the payoff of not overreacting?

Did others seem to notice the change in your actions? This should be much more than a yes-or-no response.

How did you feel about making a better choice? Be careful not to give this question the brush-off. It's a key question.

If I were to make a plan for how to get this area of my life under control, what would that plan look like? This question will take a considerable amount of space and thought. You might want to give it a few days. Write, think, meditate, dream, write some more.

There is no time like the present for instituting the plan. Let's execute it now and check in during a later section of the book about how we feel as a result.

Doing Nothing Is Often the Best Solution

It's not easy to make the choice to do nothing. Perhaps that's because doing nothing doesn't feel like an actual choice. But it is and, in fact, quite often a very wise one. Trying to force a solution to any kind of problem doesn't allow for the quiet time necessary to hear the guidance that will surely come from the God of one's understanding. Had I not *succumbed* to the choice to do nothing but pause and breathe deeply when my professor said my dissertation had to be completely rewritten, I very well might not have completed my doctorate. Doing nothing was, in all honesty, not my first choice. I simply didn't act on the first inclination, which taught me a great lesson.

It took many years of maturity for me to acquire the wisdom to do and say nothing. In my family of origin, I fought many unwinnable battles. No one was helped by them, even though I was convinced I needed to stand my ground in my arguments with my dad. I didn't quit fighting until long after I left home, in fact. My father and I had perfected our "dance," and one of us always managed to start it. Politics or people, music or entertainment, history or values were the typical triggers. Or anything else that might come up at the dinner table or during the evening news broadcast. My heart and then my temper were engaged as soon as my dad spoke harshly to my brother or my mom. It was a common and frequent theme. In time, fortunately, I came to understand that his humiliation of others was because of his own fear of humiliation, an experience he'd had to survive more than once in childhood, but at that time, I simply thought he was mean and insensitive. I'd seethe inside until my rage got the best of me, and then I'd let it spew forth.

I am very grateful that I eventually learned I didn't have to respond to everything that was said. Or even anything that was said. The decision to say nothing, regardless of the inclination to be engaged, was a mere thought away. I only wish I had learned it sooner. Fortunately I did learn it before my father died. The last few years of his life were far more peaceful for both of us. His ways didn't change very much, and that didn't matter. Mine did, and it only takes one to quit the dance for it to end.

Let me be clear, my father wasn't a bad man. He was a respected member of our community and a banker. He was simply a fear-filled man, and fear can drive anyone to behavior that can have unfortunate repercussions. I'm sure he didn't reveal his fear and concomitant anger on his job, which is probably why we saw so much of it at home. He needed to unload it, and there we were.

Not having to respond to the behavior of others, any of the behavior, is remarkably freeing. A huge burden is lifted every time we choose silence. Celebrating our powerlessness over others is a learned choice. At least it was for me. My natural inclination had always been to strike back. The true blessing in this choice is that it empowers us. Doing nothing empowers us! I was immensely surprised to discover this.

As I've heard so many times in Al-Anon, there are two kinds of business: my business and none of my business. Discerning which is yours, and paying attention to *only that,* changes how every minute feels. Not having to wonder about getting involved releases the tension that so commonly accompanies us on our journey. What great shorthand this is for living one day, one minute at a time.

Have you ever practiced making this choice between the two kinds of business? I try to do it every day. It's truly a simple question, and the answer is always quite obvious. For instance, if your friend calls, angry over something that happened to her on the job or even with her spouse at home, you don't have to make it your business to tell her what she should do. Listening, being a witness to her pain, is all that's ever "required." And it's not even required, of course, but having a kind friend to listen to our woes, as long as we don't dwell on them and live encumbered by them for days on end, is helpful.

Another good example is choosing to take a backseat and remaining quiet rather than taking sides in an argument between friends. Even if one friend wants to engage us in taking their side in the disagreement, wisdom dictates silence. We will not help them or ourselves by picking the "right" solution to a disagreement that is clearly none of our business.

None of My Business

I'd like for you to take a few moments now to think about the most recent times you got involved in the business of others. Let these questions guide your thoughts and your responses. If it helps to meditate first on each question before delving into the memory, please do so.

Why were you engaged so easily in someone else's business? This can be a tricky question.

Who did it involve? Was there anything in particular about this person that "snagged" you?

How was your interference received? If not well, how did you handle that?

If you didn't actually get involved, but wanted to, how did your desire to do so make you feel? This can be a slippery question. Don't let your response be slippery, too.

Does the choice of walking away, or at least remaining quiet, have any appeal? I suggest you practice this exercise before you go any further in the book. Keep track of the next two or three times you refrain from getting involved when it is clearly not your business. Then take time to write how that felt. This question is tied to the one that follows. If it's easier, answer both together.

How was your noninvolvement received?

What have you learned from your observations and from practicing the new behavior? Enjoy this writing section. Giving ourselves a pat on the back is good.

What do you plan to do the next time a situation seems to cry for your attention? Make a clear plan for yourself. Write it here.

Disengaging from Chaos

Chaos is everywhere. Turn on the television or talk radio, and we are bombarded. Regardless of the program, people are frequently hollering to be heard, certain that their perspective on whatever "newsworthy" event under their consideration is correct.

However, chaos isn't always loud and argumentative. It can be subtle, far quieter, and often is. The unspoken but profoundly felt tension in a home is chaos of another kind. This form of chaos, which may be the more frequent kind in your home, is insidious and eats at our inner emotional core, making it nearly impossible to ever feel a sense of well-being within the home.

And then there's the chaos that runs rampant in the workplace, where differing opinions on how to accomplish the goals of an organization pit worker against worker. This kind of chaos often goes home with the workers and infects the atmosphere there, too. And if that home atmosphere is already tense, no one can find solace.

My point is that *any discussion between any two or more people can become chaotic in the blink of an eye.* All it takes is for one of the parties in the conversation to overreact to something that's being said. And quite often, that something is part of a recollection from the person's past. Allowing the baggage of earlier years, be it minor or hefty baggage, to impede the relationships of this day, this moment, results in a mind that's trapped in chaos. We simply can't allow ourselves to be held hostage to unnecessary chaos, and nearly every experience that isn't peaceful can imprison us in a flash.

What I suggest, however, is an alternative to getting ensnared by the chaos that is all around us. It's ever so simple. Detach. Walk away. Turn to thoughts of God. Pray quietly for the benefit of someone else, *anyone else.*

Turn off the television or the radio. If it's a family member in the home who is fully engaged in chaos and who hopes to hook you, too, remove your body or at least your mind from the noise. There is a great saying that helps me if I'm in the midst of someone else's chaos: *I can see peace instead of this*. Repeating this as often as necessary, much like we repeat the Serenity Prayer when in need of it, can change how we feel or how the situation looks, and it can even diffuse the tension felt by all the parties to the chaos.

Remember, it takes our agreement to become a party to or ensnared by someone else's "insanity." The *bait* doesn't have to hook us. As I heard it said at a recent Al-Anon meeting, "Remember, we are not fish." The tools for maintaining our sanity while in the midst of the insanity of others are all around us. It's a simple choice to pick one of them up. A new habit can only be formed one choice at a time.

One of the additional payoffs from detachment, or disengagement from the noise of the chaos, is that we are setting a good example for others when we do this, and one good example can lead to many imitators. The more who imitate a good example, the more the world around us will change.

We can't expect to change everything about ourselves overnight. This is a choice-by-choice process, but every time we pick up a peaceful tool and apply it to the chaos, *rather than adding to the chaos,* we are softening the rough edges around our hearts and the hearts of all who might be within earshot or view. It simply feels good to live from a peaceful place. And it's so much easier, too.

Responding to Chaos

It's my guess that chaos has trapped you on occasion, maybe even recently. Let's take a look at some of those times here so we can see where the pitfalls are.

What triggered the most recent time you felt engaged, perhaps even enraged, by chaos? Give a few details.

Did you let it take over your emotions? If so, how did that feel, and how did you reclaim your equilibrium?

What's the most common example of chaos that ensnares you? The television, the radio, friends, coworkers, or family members? Provide some details of how a few scenarios looked.

Have you figured out some ways to take care of yourself so that you aren't held hostage by the chaos of others? List them and then give an example of exactly what you would do in particular situations.

Write an affirmation or two that you can practice before, during, and after a chaotic situation has occurred. For instance:

I am free and need not be controlled by this event, this person, or this inner turmoil.

I am not a hostage to others' behavior, now or ever.

My life is my own. No one has charge of how I feel or what I do but me.

Freedom is good. Chaos is not freedom.

Now write yours:

_____

_____

_____

Don't Take Things Too Seriously

What a relief to be reminded by good friends (and it takes a good and brave friend to do it) that we need not overreact to the common, ordinary situations that occur on a daily basis. As a matter of course, reacting, rather than making a calm choice to simply act, would describe many of us. And the situation that inspires the reaction is most often not even worth your attention, let alone a reaction.

Being too serious or overreactive is often the result of being so self-absorbed that it results in having a very limited perspective on life. Me, me, me is the theme of too many people's lives. This perspective needs a complete overhaul and seldom gets it unless good friends dare to offer helpful suggestions.

I was lucky in my early sobriety to have just such a friend in Rita. She stopped me in my tracks during a phone call, a story I shared earlier in this chapter. I never stopped thanking Rita for her words of truth. I needed the truth. I needed a friend who was brave enough to offer it. I needed to get off the poor-me couch and change my outlook on life if I wanted different experiences and a different outcome to some of the same old experiences.

No one can change us, just as we can change no one else. Change is a decision that must be made by each of us, but feedback from others regarding their observations of how we respond to our shared experiences might be the very suggestions or comments we need to commit to making an inventory of who we are in myriad situations.

Knowing ourselves and changing what we should so we can grow in the ways that are important is why we are here, after all. Helping one another see what might be hidden to us, in a respectful way, might well be considered one of the reasons for any two people to have found each other. At least it's an idea I find very compelling and comforting.

There is purpose to our lives, and assuredly, it's not to live trapped in problems, ours or other people's. We can, instead, define our problems as the classroom lessons that are perfect for us and those with whom we are sharing them. Whining about them or complaining to friends or strangers or refusing to address them in a calm, rational way means we are choosing to live in the problems rather than moving forward on our learning curve. We can stay stuck, if that's our preference. Or we can say to each and every one of them, "So what!"

It has become my preference in many instances to say, "So what?" rather than make a big deal of the many ordinary situations that arise, day in and day out, in my life or the life of a companion. I have found that the level of my peace is directly proportional to this decision to look away, walk away, disengage. Peace of mind is a choice, and it can't be found if we wallow in problems. That's my perspective, at least. What's yours?

Acting or Reacting

Are you taking life too seriously? What does that mean to you? Here is your opportunity to explore this more fully. This will be fun. You will be taking charge in a new way.

What's the first situation that comes to mind when you consider in retrospect that you overreacted? Did it hurt you or others?

Can you think of a time when you responded to a situation in a far quieter way and had a good outcome?

What would you consider a serious situation?

What kind of situation have you experienced that was worthy of "so what!"?

Is that, more or less, how you responded? If not, describe what you did.

What do you consider the most reasonable choices you could make to any situation?

Create a mantra for yourself that you might say before taking any action or responding to any situation.

Use this mantra for the next week, and then come back to these pages and write how it felt to take charge of your reactions in a fresh way.

let go of outcomes

**Let go of outcomes; they belong to the future,
and they are never yours anyway. Our "work"
is limited to our effort in every circumstance.
And the final outcome of each circumstance belongs
solely to the God of our understanding.**

So easily, even desperately, we cling to that which isn't part of our "job description." God, never us, is in charge of all outcomes. We may not like that idea, but if we can wrap our minds around it, even for one instance, we'd be able to experience how much relief and freedom it gives us. And we'd get a sense, almost immediately, of how much less burdened we are when we give up the job of trying to manage outcomes. Taking charge of others, or mistakenly thinking we are in charge of others, does more than tire us out. It frustrates us, perhaps even angers us. And it creates enemies. No one is happy when we get into minding the business of someone else.

There is a way to peacefully coexist with friends, colleagues, and family members, and we hear the advice for how to do it in many settings: "Just do the next right thing." "Let go and let God." "Do only what's in front of you now." "Don't borrow trouble from the future, your future, or anyone else's future."

I can assure you of the value of these suggestions. I had no peace of mind for the first thirty-five years of my life. Then, in 1974, I was introduced to these ideas, one by one, and I slowly began the daily practice of letting the future, everyone's future, rest solely in the hands of God.

Peace of mind, to be sustained, requires a daily commitment of "letting go," but it's one that pays a big dividend. I have been reaping the dividend ever since.

I am so grateful that I finally got the message that my work here is to attend solely to me. It's not to control anyone or anything but my own attitude, my own behavior, and my own degree of willingness to let the same be true for all my "accidental" and intentional companions. Embracing this level of freedom and detachment from all the potential "human traps" changed everything about my life: how it felt, how it appeared to others, and how it prepared me for every next moment of life. It's never too late to discover the joys of living the peace-filled life. That's what the next part of this workbook helps you discover, too.

Make Way for New Behaviors

In order to discover this kind of freedom and peace of mind, however, there are behaviors that will most likely need to change. That was certainly true in my case, as I already noted. The whole purpose of this endeavor is to become more of who we were born to be.

Let's explore the behavior(s) that might need to change. Quietly meditate on the questions before writing your responses.

How willing are you to behave responsibly, to do what you need to do but to let others take care of their own personal circumstances? In other words, do you still have an inclination to "go where you don't belong" and then to blame others for your interference? Please don't limit your response to a yes or a no.

What's the most recent irresponsible or overly responsible—that is, controlling—thing you did? Please don't simply skim the surface of your behavior. What did you do? How did it occur to you to do it?

How did it feel? Was there something you were trying to prevent or initiate?

Were you at all troubled by your behavior? Are you troubled now as you reflect on it? How did it affect those you were with at the time? Again, the more specific you can be, the more you will learn about yourself.

How do you recognize what is your responsibility and what isn't? Where does control fit into this picture? How hard is it to back away from control?

Those people on your path are present by design, whether you fail to appreciate this or not. How often do you get your effort mixed up with outcomes that clearly belong to them? How can you tell when you have crossed a line, doing or trying to do that which isn't yours to do? Offer an example or two to answer these questions. I want you to see how complicated you make your life.

In the above examples, if you were to regroup and have a redo, how would your actions look? Take a few quiet moments to sit back and dream about the redo. Then describe it fully. Enjoy the process. Creating a new vision of who you can be might well be the start of a major change in your life.

Living in the Present

Stick to what's in front of you now, and stop worrying about what might be. Joy is available only in the present. One of the biggest changes most of us need to make is letting go of the future, along with the past. Sticking with right now, right here, this moment only, is all we really have the capacity to handle. Embracing now is the solution to all our fears and anxiety. I promise you this. We kid ourselves if we think there is anything about the past that really has meaning now. And we set ourselves up for disappointment, or worse, resentment, if we look to the future for an explanation of what we could be experiencing right now. There is a gift that awaits us in each moment, and that gift is the promise of God's grace. But let me reiterate, the only way to truly experience God's grace is to stick with what's directly in front of you. In other words, don't get ahead of your nose.

This was extremely difficult for me to do for many years of my life. Certainly, before coming into twelve-step recovery, I had no clue about claiming the happiness that could be available to me if I stuck to living in the present. I was in a perpetual state of anxiety, and I owe a huge debt of gratitude to my mother-in-law for introducing me to a tiny little book by Brother Lawrence, *The Practice of the Presence of God*. He wrote in the 17th century about his constant companion, God. God was present while he was in the garden, in the kitchen, while washing dishes and setting the table. God wasn't simply present in prayer. What was true for Brother Lawrence I eventually came to believe was true for me, too.

That book gave me hope. It introduced me to the first real inkling I had of the meaning of "now." And it allowed me to look at every instant a bit more peacefully, knowing I wasn't gazing on it alone. Joy was a by-product.

Sometimes it's helpful to be quiet for a few moments before we begin the process of exploration, so let's take those few moments now. Close your eyes. Take a few deep breaths and ask God to help you in your self-examination.

Living in the Now

How would you describe to a friend what living "in the now" means? Be specific with examples from your own or someone else's life. What has been hardest for you about this concept?

Offer some examples of your successful attempts at being fully present. Is it possible to discern what made it easier in these attempts? See if you can make a crib sheet of sorts so you can repeat the process at will.

In the recently popular book *The Power of Now* by Eckhart Tolle, readers commented on how they became quietly and profoundly moved by the enchantment of "now" as the only time there is. Whether you have read the book or not, think about a time you were mystically moved by the sense of nothing existing outside the present moment. It has happened to all of us. You may need to be quiet so your memory can call it forth. When it has, savor it and then write down the details.

What's the most joyful experience you can recall? Did you share the moment with someone else? What was happening just prior to the experience? Be as detailed as you can and savor that moment here. Hanging on to our good memories helps us recognize others in the making.

Before moving on to the next topic, is there anything you haven't been prompted to write about—relating to letting go of outcomes, living in the moment, or experiencing joy—that you'd like to share? Taking an inventory of our successes in the past will help us with the blueprint we are formulating now for more sustained success in all aspects of our lives from this day forth.

changing our minds

**Being willing to change our minds in the midst
of a seemingly unchangeable experience or set
of circumstances is what real growth is all about.
It's the door opener, in fact.**

Being willing to change our minds, which means our thoughts, in all our
affairs is the next major hurdle. And we can do it!

A Course in Miracles, a spiritual training made popular in the late
1970s by Jerry Jampolsky and then in the 1980s by Marianne William-
son, introduced me to the idea of shifting my perception to ease tension
during a difficult situation. *A Course in Miracles* says that the shift is the
"miracle," and it's one that is accessible to everyone and can change how
we see every aspect of our lives from this moment forward.

Even though this idea may be unfamiliar to you, I think it's a rather
unique and simple tool for immediate application. For instance, when in a
conversation with friends or mere acquaintances, perhaps even strangers,
we often discover that we don't share the same opinion about the subject
matter under discussion. For some of us (and I admit guilt here), the red
flag begins to wave at this point. In the old days, I felt it was my job, then
and there, to convince others that however I saw the situation was the right
way to see it. I wasn't much fun to be around. My argumentativeness was
straight out of the rulebook I grew up with in my family of origin. Giving up the propensity to argue hadn't occurred to me. Being right was the
point of every conversation, I thought. My fragile self-esteem demanded it.

Living in a constant state of agitation is where a perspective like mine ultimately takes you. I watched my dad live there for more than eighty years. He wasn't a peaceful man—ever. His fists were generally clenched, his teeth, too. And I was repeating the pattern. Fortunately, I became open to living another way. I'm quite convinced that's why *A Course in Miracles* crossed my path. When the student is ready, the teacher appears, and I became that willing student, and little about my life has remained the same.

But how do we make the change, the shift, I'm talking about? That's where I take you next. It's really quite simple, as I already said. It demands willingness, however, and we have to do more than give lip service to willingness. We have to be ready to give up our knee-jerk reactions to what others say. We don't have to agree with them—and won't much of the time—but we can learn to hold our thoughts and refrain from responding. We can learn to ask the Higher Power of our understanding for help to remain quiet, and we can make the tiny request to see the situation or the person differently. Perhaps you are thinking it can't be as simple as this. But I assure you, it is.

Shift Your Perception

Changing our thoughts can be as easy as A, B, C. And that's the key to creating a different set of experiences that leads to the different life many of us deserve. One of my favorite ideas from *A Course in Miracles* is that we can and should *substitute any thought we are harboring that wouldn't please God with one that would.* This makes our choice of thoughts pretty simple. I consider it a shortcut to living the peaceful life, in fact. How we feel and see and think about our world is up to us. And only us.

Let's try an experiment. You no doubt have at least one person in your life who irritates you. I certainly do. Close your eyes for a moment and think of him or her. Think of the most recent time you were irritated by something that happened with this person. Now, draw into your heart a fond memory of you and a friend who seldom, if ever, irritates you. Now ask God to help you be willing to see the heart of each, seeing them both joyful, seeing them helping others and each other, too. Now watch yourself smiling on the two of them.

How do you feel inside after doing this experiment? Reflect and then write about this "interior" experience. I want you to feel and see the change within you.

What was the first thing that was on your mind when you woke up this morning?

If it was something positive, terrific. Savor that thought for recollection at a later time. If it was a form of grumbling, whether shared or simply quietly protected, what thought might you replace those thoughts with now?

If your first thought this morning wasn't negative or if you can't remember what you were thinking, what negative thought troubled you recently? With eyes closed, revisit that thought. This will help you understand it so you can release it. Remember, "As we think, so we are." What prompted the thought?

Is it a recurring thought? If so, when do you recall it first troubling you?

Have you tried to release it in the past unsuccessfully? If so, using what method?

Let's try this new method now: Quietly ask the God of your under-standing to help you release the thought that wouldn't please Him. (It's also one that doesn't help you, remember.) And choose one you know would please Him. For instance, what's the first loving thought that comes to your mind?

Hold on to this thought for a few minutes. Share here what happens in your mind when you do this exercise. Does this exercise inspire you to think and behave differently? It should. If it doesn't, practice again and again until it does. You deserve peace of mind. We all do. And there is only one way we can be assured of getting it.

Since what we think determines our behavior and our level of peace, what ideas do you want to savor right now? List them here.

Now take each of the above ideas and create a short scenario that reflects that you understand how the idea would change your experience of life. We need to see what life can be like in order to make the commitment to changing anything about it.

The Magnetic Power of Imagination

One of the stories I shared in *Change Your Mind and Your Life Will Follow* detailed an experience I had prior to taking my final orals for my doctorate. I was a subscriber to *Psychology Today* at the time, and about six weeks prior to the exam, I read an article about the power of envisioning ourselves performing some activity of our personal journey. This particular article chose skiers who were preparing for the Olympics as an example of the effectiveness of this "power." The trainers selected some of the skiers to do their typical rigorous skiing practices day in and day out on the mountain runs. They chose another group to sit in quiet meditation a number of times a day, envisioning themselves making the runs down the mountain, each time very successfully.

At the Olympic trials, those skiers who had sat in quiet meditation outperformed their teammates. The obvious question was, Why? The conclusion of the psychologists was that seeing ourselves performing flawlessly makes a flawless performance more likely. We repeat what we have done already.

I loved this article, and it gave me an idea. I would sit in quiet meditation for a few minutes at least twice daily until my orals. In the meditation, I could see myself in the room where I knew the orals would be held. I shook hands with the committee before beginning, and then I watched myself listen, smile, and respond to each question as it was posed. I observed my committee members smiling, too. And then we shook hands again at the end.

On the day of the exam, I walked into the room where all six of them sat, confident that we had been through this already. And indeed we had. The experience mirrored my meditation in every aspect. When it was over, I was ushered outside and told to wait for the results. The door opened, and Mr. Sibley, my chairman, motioned for me to enter. Smiling, they gave me a round of applause. Imagination is powerful, indeed.

Freedom from Fear

Now I want you to explore the power of your imagination. What is one fear or upcoming experience that seems to be holding you hostage right now? Write about the experience or the fear. Give some details so you can see the many elements from which you want freedom.

Where do you think this fear came from? Did one thing in particular initiate it, or is it more all encompassing than that?

Describe how it feels for it to hold you hostage. What's the worst part of this feeling?

If you were not ensnared by it, how might you feel most days? Is it worth doing some work to get to a different place?

Now find a quiet corner in your home. Preferably a space that is cozy and comforting to you and one where you'll not be interrupted. Turn off your cell phone, close the door if there is one, and ask family members to respect your time of meditation. Now close your eyes. Empty your mind. Slowly begin to see yourself as you want to be in the situation you have chosen. We will stay in this meditation for twenty minutes if possible. After you meditate, write about your experience here.

Were you able to quiet your mind easily?

If not, were the thoughts that came up related to what you want to change? If not, why do you think these particular thoughts emerged? Any idea?

What is the situation you want to experience more successfully? What are some specific ideas you can create around this situation that you can implant in your mind for your next meditation? It's not cheating to do this. In fact, it's one of the tools. Remember the skiers and my oral!

I quite specifically drew a positive picture in my mind, and then I kept replaying it until the day of the exam. I want you to do the same. Describe it here.

How do you feel with this new picture of possibility in your mind? How do you think it will impact your life in the immediate present and in the future, too?

Before moving on to the next chapter, I want you to stop and consider all the tools we have talked about in these first four chapters.

What tool has brought the most value to your life so far? Can you give some examples of where you used it? Go back and review where you have been.

Where do you have more work to do with one of the tools? It's not about perfection, but it is about progress. Where there is more progress to be made, let's go for it. Offer some details here of work you plan to do. I don't really want you to move forward if you can improve some of these skills that have been outlined. Be specific. This is your growth, your life, your divinity.

If you are satisfied, turn now to the next chapter.

choose your reactions

**Having spent a life reacting to the people
or circumstances in my life, I finally learned
that knee-jerk reactions are door closers.
No growth waits for us there.**

The default position of many, when in the company of a person who is getting under our skin, dismissing us altogether, or being rude or mean-spirited is to angrily or disgustedly react rather than to make a conscious choice to act. There are myriad ways to act, to respond to any situation, however. My years in Al-Anon have given me a handbook of good choices, in fact. Anger, for instance, is never one of the better ones, even when someone attacks us verbally. If the attack is physical, there is only one sensible response: get out of the vicinity of the attacker immediately.

Because our choices make the difference in the kind of day we will have, let's review what some of the common but unfortunate choices are. To begin with, anger is a poor one, and so is the silent treatment when it is accompanied by sullenness. Let me be clear, however: There is a difference between silence and the silent treatment. Choosing to say nothing in the face of someone else's anger, disrespect, or behavior that is clearly designed to rile us up is an excellent response. Respectfully leaving the room, walking away from a situation that looks like a setup for a fight, is also a good choice. If there is a need to say something in that moment, and sometimes there is, why not let it be "I'd rather discuss this at a later time"? Or perhaps an even better response is to say, "My opinion is different from yours, but we can agree to disagree." A gentle response is always an effective one. Another one I have used frequently is "I know you are perceiving this situation differently than I see it, and that's fine."

There are those occasions when we choose, unfortunately, a reaction that is designed to control what the other person might be feeling or thinking. Or even worse than that, we let what we assume the other person is feeling define how we suddenly feel, about them, ourselves, and the rest of the day. I was stunned when I read a few passages in *Why Am I Afraid to Tell You Who I Am?*, a book by John Powell a few years ago that illustrates this point. He was with a friend, and they were purchasing a newspaper from a vender on the streets of New York. The vender was gruff, very rude, and generally dismissive. Powell's friend was very kind anyway, even giving the man a tip. When Powell asked him why he chose to be kind, his response was "Why should I let the vendor decide what kind of day I am going to have?" What a mind-jarring moment that was for me.

That had been the story of my life. What you did, how you treated me, whether you paid attention to me or dismissed me determined how I felt on a moment-by-moment basis. As a consequence, I seldom felt empowered or content or worthy—certainly never peaceful in a sustained way. I was always watching you to see if I was okay. What an empty, isolated way to live. Sound familiar? But then came Al-Anon and a plethora of new choices for responding to everyone and every circumstance. I relish the choices I have been given, and I love sharing them with others.

No More Knee-Jerk Reactions

Let's delve more specifically into your choices and reflect on how they have played out, or not, in your life.

Was there recently a time or two when you overreacted to someone? How did that look, and how did you feel afterward? Was the person a friend or a stranger? Did who the person was affect you more or less adversely?

Make a plan for a way to respond that isn't a knee-jerk reaction. Use the space here to re-create one recent scene in which you had a knee-jerk reaction, and replay it in a more effective, respectful way.

What's the first observation you can make about the redo? Did you feel different? Can you see how thinking first, pausing perhaps, can change the tenor of your life?

Knee-Jerk Reactions Prevent the Peaceful Life

Choosing another way to react, even if it feels awkward at first, will comfort you and everyone around you, too. Perhaps we have to reach the stage of maturity I am in to desire this, but peace is worth seeking, regardless. I want peace of mind. I want quiet, peaceful relations with others, no matter where those others cross my path—at home, in the grocery store, or among friends. What I have come to understand and cherish is that every encounter I have that I respond to peacefully benefits me and all my other encounters throughout the day. I personally think it benefits the planet, too.

I'm quite convinced that the seduction to get involved in the business of others is rooted in our insecurities. For instance, if you have business that doesn't include me, perhaps a social engagement with friends, does that mean you might be leaving me behind? This was one of my typical obsessions before I got into a spiritual program of recovery. I placed all my focus on others, what they were doing, what I assumed they might be thinking, whether or not they were thinking about me in the hours I was wondering about them. My attempts at control gave my life meaning and security, I thought. Letting others live their own lives, follow their own path, and have their own opinions, dreams, and goals was a terrifying idea. My need to cling and to be in charge was all consuming. And completely insane.

The concept of detachment—how to do it, how it looked, and what it offered as a new way of life—was mind altering, particularly when my life, since childhood, had been about attachment. Not letting others have a life of their own was my job, as I've already noted. I took it very seriously. That it implied I didn't have a life of my own had never occurred to me. We were enmeshed, and I loved it that way.

Hearing about the joys of detachment, letting others be in charge of their own lives, simply didn't register as desirable or, in all honesty, even possible. And yet I heard men and women sing the praises of detachment all the time. I figured I might as well give it a try, but how?

What I quickly discovered was that my connection to the God of my understanding needed strengthening if I was ever to claim a working understanding of detachment. The only way to "detach," to let go, was to take the next step and "let God." Letting God be in charge of my life and everyone else's, too, was the solution to my obsessive thinking. Practice was the requirement, I discovered. Perhaps some people can learn to trust their loved ones to God in one attempt, but that wasn't true for me.

Making the commitment to let God do his work while I attended to mine felt empowering. But I have had to remain committed to this practice regardless. Even though I no longer feel scared about someone leaving my life when I let them go, I know it's because I stay attached to God, rather than to them. And I count my many blessings for all my lessons along the way, including, perhaps, the most powerful one of all: remember, there are two kinds of business, my business and none of my business.

Look at the Business of Your Life

Unless you have lived more successfully than many of us, you may have found yourself minding someone else's business as recently as yesterday. That wouldn't be unusual, in fact. That you chose this book to read suggests that you might want help with this issue. It's my hope to offer it. In order to do that, we need to inventory your behavior. I have to look at my own every day. When I feel any amount of tension between me and someone else, I see that as an indication that I may have stepped over the boundaries between my life and theirs. Facing that, addressing it, and changing it is what growth, leading to the peace-filled life, is about. I hope the following questions guide you to make some important discoveries about yourself.

When did you most recently stick your nose into business that wasn't yours? How did your companion or spouse or friend respond? Did your "effort" prove satisfying? Explain.

How would you describe minding your own business? Offer an example.

Re-create the recent experience you discussed in the first question, demonstrating the principle we are trying to master here.

One of the most effective ways we can practice being hands-off is to see ourselves placing those loved ones who are journeying with us in the hands of God. Take a few moments now to close your eyes and envision that image. Keep this thought and the accompanying feeling it gives you close to your heart so you can resurrect it at will. Share some of the feelings here.

Others' Mood Swings Don't Determine Your Emotional State

Taking responsibility for ourselves, our actions, and our feelings rather than foisting this responsibility onto others is one of the hallmarks of emotional maturity. However, blaming the mood swings of others for our diminished self-esteem is a common response.

I'm sorry to say it's a response that I practiced for many decades. Growing up in a dysfunctional home with an angry, insecure father and a generally depressed mother didn't prepare me for handling with any clarity the emotions of the hundreds of others I was destined to meet over the years. As a child, I was sure that if I did things differently, I could make them happy. As I got older, I saw this wasn't the case, so I rebelled, which only worsened every situation with them.

The sadness, however, is that I developed a grooved habit of letting the behavior of all others define me. I was a chameleon. If you were happy, I was relieved and secure. If you were angry, I tried to change your mood for my own benefit. If you distanced yourself from me for any reason, I panicked. If you were dismissive, I showered you with attention, trying to get you back "in the fold." How I felt was totally the result of how you saw me. And then I was introduced to Al-Anon.

I've visited this idea already, but it's too important not to mention again. Without the principles of twelve-step recovery, I'd still be struggling to live a whole, free, and peaceful life. I entered Al-Anon in 1974 feeling hopeless about every relationship and the direction of my life. I was terrified of abandonment, rejection, anger, and failure, and I was bereft of all purpose.

I was told to "keep coming back," and eventually there was a crack in this wall of darkness. Little by little, I let the words of others penetrate my mind, and I heard them say they were no longer controlled by the mood swings of others. I found that unimaginable, but I was willing to be willing to listen and learn. The rest is history, as they say.

How Others' Mood Swings Affect You

Looking at how the mood swings of others affect you will be a fun exercise. It will be edifying, too, as well as life changing.

What's the first thing you do when you observe a mood that isn't loving, welcoming, and kind? Give some recent examples.

If what you pointed out in the question above doesn't actually make you proud, how would you have preferred to behave?

If you thought your behavior was affecting other people, as others' behavior has affected you in the past, what might you do differently?

While it's true we can't control others by our behavior, we can encourage happiness by treating others in a kind way. Give an instance of when you might have approached a person or a situation differently. Paint the scene clearly for your own growth.

What is your most common mood? What do you do to maintain it, if it's good, or change it if it's bad?

give up negative judgments

Giving up negative judgments can change the tenor of your life. Completely. And immediately.

Being judgmental, holding another person hostage to your negative mind-set about him, creates a prison cell that encloses both of you. But before saying more, I do want to draw an important distinction between being judgmental, which is never to the benefit of anyone, and making sound judgments about the many situations and people in our lives.

Sound judgments make good sense. They quite properly prevent us from making many of the mistakes our ego might find attractive. They guide us to healthy living. Sound judgments help us make good decisions about choices in friends, jobs, investments, and life partners. But being judgmental about others, about others' actions, their opinions, their appearance, or their goals or dreams, is very small-minded. And it implies grave insecurities about ourselves.

A phrase that I hear often is "You spot it, you got it," meaning, what I see in you is a reflection of a quality in me. I hated that phrase the first time I heard it. I was a master at being judgmental. And I certainly didn't want to claim any of the characteristics for myself that I so easily sniped about in others. It took me some time, coupled with a lot of willingness, to understand the full implication of the phrase.

Our ego lies to us and wants to undermine us. That's its primary purpose, I think. Seeing others in a poor light is how we elevate ourselves and search for security, and it's a choice the ego makes. I'm ashamed to say it was a habit I had to work very hard to break. And I'm still quite capable of elevating myself at the expense of others. I know that when I do, it's time for a "housecleaning." Something is going on within that I need to address. Most often it's a sign that my friendship with the God of my understanding needs attention. For me, staying connected to God, walking securely on the spiritual path, is an activity that must be at the center of my life on a daily basis.

But what does that mean? Honoring God, acknowledging His presence in my life, didn't come naturally to me. It wasn't that I came into the twelve-step rooms kicking and screaming in 1974. On the contrary, I was eager—desperate, in fact—to learn how to control others so that I'd feel secure, so that I wouldn't feel neglected or compelled to judge others for their behavior. Alas, that wasn't the formula offered. Getting to know God, and then trusting all my companions to His care, was.

What a turn my life has taken from that spring evening forward. As I sit here today, writing this book, my twenty-sixth, I'm profoundly amazed. This was not the picture I had imagined for my life. No indeed. Yet it couldn't feel more perfect. More blessed. More peaceful. And there is one reason, and only one reason, for the change in my attitude: I developed a trust in God. I gave Him my journey and everyone else's, too. I realized that those whom I walked among were there as my teachers—not to be judged, but from whom I could learn. And my heart opened.

When we begin to look at the companions on our path as our teachers, we are less inclined to judge them negatively, or if we do judge them, we know it's a sign that it's time to look at ourselves. Life is full of opportunities for changing ourselves. Let's consider now the many opportunities that being judgmental has given us.

Negative judgments of others diminish us. In order to be rid of them, we must first acknowledge them.

Acknowledging Negative Judgments

What does being judgmental mean to you? Is there a specific clue that alerts you to the presence of this attitude?

Can you think back to a time when you were less judgmental? If so, what made you freer then? If you were to recapture that feeling, how would you attempt it?

Our judgments, like our secrets, keep us stuck. Which judgments are holding you back right now?

Can you see progress in your life in regard to this trait? Because it's important to acknowledge our progress, journal about it here as a reminder of where you were and where you now are.

Unconditional Love

Before moving on, let me say that the opposite of negative judgment is unconditional love, the kind of love that the God of our understanding has for us. It's the goal of this undertaking here that we learn how to offer unconditional love rather than criticism, judgment, or dismissive behavior toward our fellow travelers. Today is the right day to begin the change that will influence the remainder of our lives. The question is, are you truly ready?

Without changing ourselves, we will always show up as we always did, and nothing about our relationships will be different. The real work has to begin sometime. We have been making some changes ever since beginning this book, but we aren't done. And I see that as the good news, actually. Change is good. It means we are still progressing. Still willing. Still teachable. Stopping the behavior of judging others not only lifts our spirits, but like so many of the other changes I am suggesting in this book, it also benefits many others in the process.

What We Do to One, We Do to All

This is a spiritual axiom that has profound consequences. What it means is that my treatment of you has a ripple effect. If the treatment is unkind, which has developed from negative judgment, those on the receiving end will be less likely to shower kindness on the next person they see. What goes around keeps getting passed on. The idea is to "pay forward" good thoughts, good behavior, and good wishes on behalf of others.

Let's take some time here to see how we are measuring up. It's terribly important to acknowledge our changed behavior within key relationships. We never quit needing affirmation, our own or someone else's.

Think of the most important relationship currently in your life. When it's at its worst, how would it appear to someone observing it? Give as complete and as unbiased description of it as you can.

What would you like these observers to see instead? Paint that picture in words here.

_____

_____

_____

We spoke of unconditional love a bit earlier. If you were expressing this kind of love, rather than making unkind judgments about your dearest friend, describe how changed a recent experience with him or her might look.

_____

_____

_____

Share anything else about being judgmental that has resulted in tension in a relationship, or worse.

_____

_____

_____

Rooting Out Fear

Rooting out the fear that can undermine our very lives and thus every relationship, too, is the necessary first step to being able to experience the lives we deserve, the lives we are supposed to have, and the relationships that complement those lives.

Where we go next is to our toolbox of solutions. There are many solutions, and some will work better in some instances than others will. Some will work well in all. Let's take them one at a time and measure how we are doing with each one currently. Then we'll project how the picture might look if we were to be very successful in wielding the tool.

The number one tool for freedom from fear is always faith, but how we get it is often the problem. My way, and it doesn't have to be yours, is to remember that everyone I walk among is here by divine appointment. God is part of every dynamic. I don't question that. It's a fact that I take on faith.

> How about you? How would you describe your faith when it comes to the topic of relationships? Focus particularly on the one or two that are the most significant at the present time.

Another tool, so to speak, is *remembering* that our companions are our intentional learning partners. I have mentioned this concept earlier in the book, but emphasizing it again here can offer a lot of relief, I think. "Intentional" means you have work to do together. That's why you are sharing this space in time.

> Name some of your intentional partners.

> What have been some of the obvious lessons of your relationships with these partners?

> Which ones have you yet to comfortably absorb?

Is there an intentional learning partner whose intended lesson you have not yet been able to face? Explain why you think that is.

Before moving forward, create a blueprint for how to handle or resolve or get free of the lesson that has you in its grip. There is a reason it has "come calling." Don't try to escape it. It will follow you.

This entire exercise has been about judgments and the lessons they embody and how they hinder us or even imprison us. The section has also been about how to get free of them and why getting free is so important for our many loved ones as well as for the planet. Let's meditate for a few minutes about those judgments that *used to be* at the core of our being, taking particular note of how freedom from them feels.

In one brief paragraph, fifty words or less, describe the feeling of freedom.

Choosing Peace

Choosing peace over the need to be right is a step in the right direction if we want relationships that bless us as well as those we love. This seems like a tall order. It begins with a decision, however, and not a particularly major one. It's a decision that says I will not be engaged in a conversation that is moving in "this" direction. Or perhaps it's a decision where you simply say, "You might be right," to the person intent on having a conversation that has no easy resolution.

Every conversation that engages us has one thing in common. It's offering us an opportunity to express love and acceptance and perhaps, on occasion, forgiveness. But every one of the encounters, as I've said in other places, has been "planned for" already. More than likely, we have no recollection of the plan. Caroline Myss, the spiritual intuitive I have referenced before, says we make the plan before arriving here, *in these skins, to live these lives.* We then draw one another to us. And the lessons unfold.

Making Peaceful Choices

I, for one, treasure the many lessons, though hindsight was needed along the way. But I think I can say quite honestly that the choice for peace over needing to be right has had the most profound impact of all the lessons to which I stay committed. The good news is that there are many avenues of behavior that foster peace over being right. Some I have explained already, and there are no doubt many more that I haven't listed here, but the following list gives you an overview of some of the peaceful, sensible choices for responding to the "teachers" on your path. We can never give too much attention to the search for peace. Short-changing ourselves will short-change everyone else on our path, too. The reason for this exercise is that we need to see how we might do something differently and practice the new choice, at least in our minds. Exploring the more positive, peaceful feelings will give us reason to want to make the new behavior permanent.

Take each choice, one by one, and talk about a real experience where this response would have been beneficial.

Saying nothing in the face of minor agitation or unmistakable anger or an act of control from someone else fosters inner peace.

Leaving the room when voices reach a fever pitch is a wise response.

Deciding to agree with one's counterpart rather than prolonging an unwinnable battle is a fair choice.

Make a gratitude list each evening for the many "resolutions" that were accomplished during the day.

At the start of the new day, reread yesterday's list following morning prayers.

Appreciate every relationship along with every simple encounter as the sole opportunity you have for acting the way God wants you to act.

Never forget that you will not be sent only those people who are easy to love. The real lessons in life reside in the encounters with those who are hard to love.

What's the overall feeling you have as the result of this exercise? Are you getting the results you had hoped for from this book?

What's the primary change you can claim so far?

accept the gift of powerlessness

We are powerless over others. Hallelujah.

Being compulsively obsessed with trying to control what others are doing, thinking, saying, planning, and dreaming about is deadly to one's spirit. Unfortunately it's an obsession of tens, perhaps hundreds of millions of people. And never will we experience peace in our own lives if we are focused exclusively on the details of other people's lives. The attraction to watch others may be strong, for sure—we are nosey, after all—but the growth each of us is here to experience can be realized only if we mind our own business and seek to embrace God's will for us, and only us.

A great shorthand bit of philosophy to remember when you're attracted to the chaos of others' lives is this: if you want a peaceful life, you must be engaged in peaceful behavior. Trying to control the uncontrollable—and everything but your own life is out of your control—is futile. And it's definitely not peaceful behavior. I have explored this idea with you in an earlier section, but it's of paramount importance and worth looking at again. We are drawn into the tiny details of others' lives primarily for two reasons: we want to avoid some issue in our own life (and we must discern what this is) or we want to prevent the person who is the focus of our attention from getting away.

Believing that we can't control others, even if we don't think it's true, is the healthiest mind-set we can cultivate. It frees us from the constant nagging our minds are capable of when they push us to do the undoable. And remember, anyone you are intent on controlling and keeping as your hostage will escape. Every time.

There is only one sensible plan of action. Back away from your loved ones' lives. Let them go. Trust the God of your understanding to watch over you and them. Their journey, as I have stated so many times, is woven into yours, to be sure, but that does not mean it's for you to control. They are following their own set of "Godly" directions. It's your assignment to do the same. The thrill of looking at it from this perspective is that life becomes an adventure. You have more time to focus on your adventure if you let your loved ones do the same. Their choices may lead to simple mistakes or worse, but that's part of their journey, one they "selected," as you'll recall, and for you to intervene means you are preventing their destiny from unfolding as it should. Celebrating this perspective, as I choose to do daily, has made my life quieter, definitely free from anxiety, and knowingly intentional. Can you say this about yours?

Trying to control anyone else is a huge burden to carry. Put it down. Now. Feel the freedom that immediately comes with accepting what is rather than trying to force what can never be. The more quickly you unburden yourself, the sooner you will discover the peaceful life that every one of us deserves. What's true is that trying to force anything simply makes life tougher. And success will never be ours.

Envisioning Freedom

Let's look at the burdens we carry and envision freedom instead. Meditate for a few minutes about the many situations and people you are trying to control. See yourself letting them go one by one. Breathe deeply every time you let someone or something go. Sit back and let God fill your heart. Don't hurry this process. Being quiet is good.

Who or what are you letting go first? Why?

If you were to truly let this person or thing go, how might you feel? What has given rise to your resistance up to now?

How would letting go of the control affect you right now?

Describe what a "free" relationship might look like. Describe the feelings that accompany the picture you see.

Being Grateful for Powerlessness

Let me repeat, our powerlessness over others is a gift, but it's not one for which we are immediately grateful. It generally takes hindsight to see the value in the gift. At least that was true for me. I had to look back and envision what my life might have become had my first marriage not ended as it did. And I had to come to grips with where I was headed on my many escapades in the unhealthy, dangerous relationships that I found so compelling.

Toyce, my colleague at my university, was truly a godsend. I know that now. Her suggestion that I seek another path, one that included a twelve-step program, was God's plan assuredly, but I could have resisted until it was too late. Why I didn't would be a mystery if I had not come to believe that my destiny had already been selected and therefore decided. So here I am, talking to you, gratefully sharing my experience, my strength, my hope, and the little wisdom God has passed on to me. I say again, hallelujah.

Take Charge of the Effort, Not the Outcome

I want you to claim and then celebrate your powerlessness now, in this moment. Think of all that you know you are powerless to control. See each of those situations, those people, those possibilities for the future as part of God's domain, not yours. Remember, we are in charge of the effort, not the outcome. Close your eyes and envision everyone traveling free of your control. Let's remain still for the next few minutes.

Describe how you feel. Are you relieved or fearful? Why?

How do you want to live now?

How will you prevent yourself from reverting to the controlling person you were? You will most likely need a plan.

See your companions as God-sent for a shared purpose. How does seeing them that way feel? List one or two of your friends and see if you can discern the shared purpose.

If you sense you are trying to control, create an affirmation to free you, and read it often, particularly before getting together with your friend. For instance:

You and I are one. We are on this shared mission.
I am here to help you. You are here to help me.
God is here to guide both of us.

Now write your own affirmation:

After practicing this exercise a few times, share in the space below the success or continuing struggle you have with letting others live freely.

This Journey Is Yours! Claim It.
Accept It. Rejoice in It.

It's far too easy to blame others for what's happening in our lives: the experiences right now or those during our childhood. It sounds harsh, perhaps, but the axiom that there are no victims, only volunteers, can be a freeing philosophy. Learning to take responsibility for everything that happens, or ever did happen, can seem daunting at first. I didn't like the sound of it when I first heard this suggestion, but because I had faith in the person who shared the idea, I trusted there might be some truth in it. And I have come to understand that accepting ourselves as volunteers, always, makes us resilient and willing learners, too. When we are blessed with both of these traits, nothing will be too much for us to handle. I can attest to that.

When I was young, I was sexually assaulted by a "family" member, not someone from the immediate family but a person who was often on the scene, nonetheless. I never felt safe in sharing what was happening with others. I was afraid of being blamed or not believed. So like many young girls, I said nothing. It happened more than once, and I was haunted by the experiences, certain they would infect my life in some way. Of course they did. The anger and accompanying unforgiveness I felt for decades impacted every relationship I had. I'm convinced that's what anger and unforgiveness always do. It wasn't until many years later that I chose to forgive the perpetrator. We never discussed it. I never revealed it to anyone in the family. But through my own prayer and openness to God's grace, I felt done with it. What I had also learned in the meantime was that I had to forgive myself as well for my many years of judgment about him. Some days it's still hard to think of myself as a "volunteer," but if I truly believe the words of Caroline Myss (and I do) that we have selected our journey and every detail and person who is on it, then I also have to see that particular time of my life as important for the forgiveness lesson it was offering me, a lesson that has been so valuable many times since then.

Let's regroup for a spell. That's a heavy recollection for me even though I have been able to forgive him. You might have something similar in your past. If so, let's see if you have freed yourself of it.

If there is a situation that troubled you in a serious way in your past, share it and how you put it to rest, if you did. And if it still troubles you, let's make a plan for putting it to rest. The remainder of your life needs to be freed from it.

Name the situation.

How did you let it go? If you haven't let it go, what can you imagine doing to prepare yourself to let it go?

I suggest you begin with a prayer for whoever was involved in the situation. Write the prayer here.

Now I suggest you create an affirmation to guide your thoughts if ever the memory of the situation arises again. Write it here.

If the situation or person still steals your peace of mind, write a letter to God and tuck it away in a God box. After a week of morning and evening prayer and repeating the affirmation multiple times daily, check the God box. You will discover the "problem" has evaporated. I promise you. Write the letter here.

Shifting Our Perception

We can be free of any obsession, any chaotic mind-set, and any compulsion to control, argue, or insist on being right or sullen or mean-spirited if we ask the God of our understanding for the willingness to see whatever there is to see from a different perspective. It's really quite simple. However, our ego mind wants to make it complicated so it can maintain control of us. But remember, we can listen to another voice. It will softly lead us to the peaceful vision that says life is good, it's perfect if left in God's hands, and it's intentional and carrying each of us to the next lesson that has been prepared for us.

As long as we live, there are still lessons. Trying to interfere with those of someone else creates the disharmony that disrupts the planet. The choice for each of us is clear. Let go. Follow your own path. Trust the God within. Let your fellow companions do likewise.

What might your remaining lessons be? Any idea? What still gets in your way of peaceful relationships? That's a clue. Think about it for a while, and then write about your observations.

What are the lessons and with whom?

How might you respond to them? Take them one at a time.

If helpful, create an affirmation or a God box prayer for help with each of them and write them here.

discover your own lessons

Discovering your own lessons, exclusive of anyone else's, requires openness, willingness, honesty, daily commitment, and a sense of purpose.

Life lessons are why we are here. It's been my experience that these lessons are most obvious within the relationships that command the bulk of our attention. As I have said in other sections of this book, I think we agreed to these particular lessons before our birth on this earthly plane, an agreement that was forgotten as soon as it was made.

But let's explore the real meat of this idea. Even though our lessons necessitate our experiences with others, *my lessons will not be the same as yours.* Getting my lessons confused with yours, as happens among friends, contributes to the enmeshment we may be guilty of creating, an enmeshment that hinders the growth that both of us are here to experience. Pointing this out is not designed to undermine the progress of either of us. It's simply to help us see how delicately our paths are woven together. We must maintain this delicate balance, this "dance," without stepping on the toes of one another. Stepping on toes is an indication of our *untreated* codependency.

I personally find it exciting to recognize, in my companions, those subtle hints of why we are traveling this path side by side. Although I have to remain vigilant against the desire to interpret your lessons and then steer them, I like knowing that the God of our understanding travels with both of us every step of the way. The bottom line is this, however: *Your life is yours. Mine is mine.* We need each other, but we aren't traveling together in order to fulfill the same exact purpose.

Let's look at that purpose next. After living seventy-two years, thirty-six of them in the rooms of AA and Al-Anon, I have been able to very clearly discern that one of my primary lessons has been to give up my desire to control all the people who cross my path. Giving up this desire has not been 100 percent successful, I might add, but having the desire to control, and acting on it, are quite separate in execution. I may *want* to control all the people around me, and I very often do want that, but *wanting to* and *actually attempting to* are not the same. From many wise men and women on my journey, I have learned the finer points of the difference between wanting and attempting.

One of my primary lessons, along with recognizing that wanting to control stems from our natural insecurities, is that I have needed to master the art of detachment. Control and detachment actually go hand in hand. But I think detaching is a more subtle response to the many personal encounters and circumstances that occur on a daily basis. I was unable to detach from any situation or person for most of the first forty years of my life. Whatever another person did impacted me to a great extent. Fortunately, I am not imprisoned by the moods and behaviors of others as a general practice any longer. However, it can still happen, and it very recently did. I want to share some of the details of my experience simply to show that our vigilance against getting ensnared by the behavior of others can never be relaxed.

Over the period of a few weeks, I was voluntarily trying to help another person on this recovery path with some issues that were troubling her. I could well understand her struggle and was hopeful that my words of encouragement, based on my own experience, strength, and hope, could be heard. What I hadn't counted on was that I would become the target of her anger, which resulted in an assault, of sorts, on me. I was caught completely off guard and suddenly felt vulnerable to her attack.

Even though I had been a practitioner, for years, of the idea that the behavior of others need not affect me or my feelings—as I've stated, one of the key lessons I've learned—I was thrown slightly off balance by the situation. While I knew her attack wasn't actually about me, I also discovered that my feelings could still be injured unless I turned to God every moment I felt under siege. My handling of it was to *bless her* every time I thought of her and to see her surrounded by the white light of God's presence.

Eventually I was able to fully hand her over to God. What I learned in the process was that, much like addiction, the inclination to let the behavior of others affect us dies a hard death. And when it's one of our primary lessons, it may continue to visit us periodically, perhaps as a recap of why we are here. Pronouncing it *good,* rather than being undermined by it, keeps our connection to God as tight as it always needs to be. I have chosen to see this experience as a simple reminder that our lessons come in many forms and every one of them adds a new thread to the tapestry of our life.

Detaching from Others

Walking among others is how life is experienced. Being focused on one life only, our own, is the peaceful way to grow. Asking yourself if the art of detachment is one of your lessons, makes sense. It's certainly one of mine.

What do you imagine is your primary lesson? Why do you think this is it? Share the evidence that this is so.

Provide some examples of how you have been tested by this lesson and how you measured up.

Most of us have many lessons. Share what you see as another one of yours and give some examples of your success in handling it.

Is being able to detach from the lives of others an issue for you? If it is, what do you see as the primary antidote to it? Share some of the times you have had success with detaching.

Repatterning Behavior

Developing new behaviors in the midst of the old patterns and chaotic circumstances is a sign of emotional maturity. That's what this journey is about. And the opportunities to "try on" new behaviors are always tied to the lessons we encounter. For instance, the unhealthy behavior of my friend that I described in the last section presented me with the opportunity to be willing to detach rather than be ensnared by it. My choice, rather than to respond at all to the behavior, was to silently pray and turn away. I had to stay committed to this choice, however. That's always part of the equation.

In years past, I would have fought back. I would have defended myself. I would have met the attack with one of my own, feeling completely justified. Now I know that there is no need to defend myself. Ever. From *A Course in Miracles* I have learned that "Every loving thought is true. Everything else is an appeal for healing and help, regardless of the form it takes." Silence in the face of someone else's storm is always far more powerful. And it is what ultimately helps to lessen the tension through-out the universe. *Silence is the new behavior that I'm cultivating,* and in the process, I'm discovering how profound it is.

When I heard a speaker at Unity Village, a spiritual center just out-side of Kansas City, Missouri, talk about this idea in the mid-1970s, I was suspect. How could what I did ever impact others on the other side of the planet? Now I doubt it not at all. Margaret Mead expressed the same idea so eloquently many years ago, too: "Never doubt that a small group of thoughtful, committed citizens can change the world. Indeed, it's the only thing that ever has." What you do to one, you do to all. This is a great shorthand way to monitor our behavior and make a significant contribution at the same time, I think.

I am well aware that my lessons are many, but they are not difficult. They all have to be practiced within the confines of the relationships into which I am drawn, however. I believe the same is true for you, too. As I've said myriad times, the reason for our relationships is the les-sons; within them is the growth we deserve. My lessons are not yours. They may be mirror images of yours, but how I learn mine may not be how you learn yours. That's why it's so very important that we allow each other the latitude that's needed for our development. We are not competing. We are teamed up, however, because both of us need the opportunity to change our lives that the presence of each of us offers to the other.

Since coming to believe that our lives are purposeful, and *intercon-necting,* the uncertainty and anxiety I used to live with has disappeared. Even within a few months of adopting this belief, I could feel the lessen-ing of my fears, and I was amazed. I had assumed, from childhood well into adulthood, that fear would be my constant companion until death. A shift in my consciousness changed all that. The realization that God had to have been present throughout my life could not be denied. It became apparent I'd not still be alive unless He existed. Having this as one of my primary lessons made all the rest of them easier to fathom.

Discovering what my lessons have been in this life has provided me with immeasurable joy coupled with hope. They have all seemed quite manageable once I carefully considered them and particularly after learning that I had agreed to them before arriving "here." That realization took the dread, shame, and fear and rightsized them. I hope the same has been true for you, but if not, it's my hope that the exercises in this book make a difference.

In order to help you discover more of your lessons, if you are in a quandary about them, let me name a few more of mine. They may trigger some awarenesses in you. I've mentioned already that one lesson has been learning to let go and let my companions control their own lives. And I've stressed, too, the importance of detaching from the behavior of everyone, friends and strangers alike. Not letting what anyone else does affect me is perhaps the lesson that has changed my life the most profoundly. Making the choice to shift my perception rather than letting any negative experience define me has proven to be "the miracle" *A Course in Miracles* promises. *Learning to mind my own business* is another lesson, one that allowed me to reap many benefits that I might not otherwise have experienced.

Being able to recount some of my lessons here, knowing that my success with them has changed my life in ways I could never have imagined possible a few decades ago, is more than a treat for me. It's the affirmation that assures me my life and the work I do is intentional and part of God's divine plan for me—and His plan for you, too, since you are reading this. Celebrating our lessons, no matter how difficult some of the concomitant experiences were or continue to be is a sign of progress and maturity.

Acknowledging Progress

Looking at where your progress has taken you is terribly important. Let's do that now.

What has changed most for you since beginning these workbook exercises?

If you have seen changes in multiple areas, and you probably have, try to rank them in order of importance, particularly as far as your peace of mind is concerned.

Generally, there is excitement that accompanies the realization that we really are changing. Hindsight is the best indicator. How valuable has hindsight been to you? How reliable has it been? Another indicator of change is feedback from friends. Ask them what they observe about you now and report their responses here.

Be a Witness Instead of a Hostage

The lessons we have been born to learn will be postponed if our minds are held hostage by the "antics" of others. Far be it from me to suggest that we shouldn't be fully aware of the many other people on our path, which of course means we will be privy to their antics. And yet, serving as the witnesses for one another is one of the highest honors we can, and should, pay. We all deserve this gift of acknowledgment, antics or not.

Many would say the gift should include the expression of kindness as well. I'm frequently reminded of a comment made by Mother Teresa many years ago. She said, and I paraphrase, "Be kind to everyone, and start with the person standing next to you." This simple suggestion, if followed by all of us, would shift the universe, making it a more peaceful, accommodating world. But this idea begs the question, can we spend too much time observing others, thus preventing us from doing the work we have been called to do? If our minds are filled with the details of the lives of others, we have no capacity to discern what is really our life, separate from them. I'm not suggesting that we emphasize being separate from our fellow travelers. Health and spiritual wholeness is encompassed in the idea of *joining with* others. But there is a distinct difference between joining with and being joined at the hip. It's the latter we must avoid. And it's the latter that is so clearly the intention of those people who are "attached" to others in codependent relationships.

Codependency is a phenomenon that is endemic among women, and occasionally men, too. I see them at Al-Anon meetings. Learning to recognize and appreciate the value of having only one life to live, *our own,* is what we stress at these twelve-step meetings. Wanting to fill our heads with the problems of others not only doesn't solve their problems but also prevents them from learning to rely on their own Higher Power, and it leaves no time for us to solve our own problems. I've always been a bit suspicious that one of the reasons we focus so intently on others is that it keeps us occupied and teases us into thinking we are participating in valuable work rather than in no work at all.

We have to ask ourselves why we work so hard to avoid our own lives. What do we fear? Is it that we'll discover we are lacking in value? Or ingenuity? Or creativity? Or intellect? Perhaps these are the reasons that apply for many, particularly those who, like was true for me for so many years, have no secure connection to a God of their understanding, the kind of connection that promises you are worthy and your life has purpose. The back cover copy on Richard Bach's *Illusions* says, "If you are reading this, it means you are still alive and have yet to fulfill your purpose." This simple bit of wisdom gave me hope nearly thirty-six years ago. And it still gives me hope. Any day that I feel at all "dis-eased," I remember that back cover copy, and I know I am still on the journey that's perfect for me.

One thing that gave my life direction and substance in the early days of recovery was learning that those who travel with us are our teachers. This idea was truly unfamiliar to me. And when a sponsor shared it with me, I was actually mystified. She was the one who also explained that we were born specifically to learn the lessons these "wandering" teachers were present to teach. I can still remember where we sat when she told me this. I felt unsettled by her words. Afraid, even. I wasn't sure, at that moment, if having her for a sponsor was good for me. My spiritual leanings were far more traditional than I was discovering was true for her. I laugh about that now. I was afraid to believe in the metaphysical explanations she offered about life but even more afraid to believe in so little. And my sponsor had many sponsees, and they all seemed to share her beliefs. I didn't want to be left out of the loop, so I joined "her group of pigeons."

Now one of the ideas I treasure the most is believing that every one of you is here to help me and vice versa. That awareness has changed how I look at all the current circumstances and people in my life and those past ones, too, that on occasion were unsettling or worse. I needed each of the experiences for the "gifts" I was scheduled to offer others. Isn't that a glorious education?

Pay Homage to Your "Teachers"

Let's take some time, now, to pay homage to the "teachers" who have shown up in our lives. None of them came forth willy-nilly. They all had "assignments," as did we. From some we learned instantly what they came to teach us. In other instances the lesson and the teacher had to be repeated a second or a third time. There was no timeline. There never will be a timeline. We can postpone until later whatever feels too much for us today.

Who are the teachers who come most quickly to mind? Let's begin with your childhood first. What were the primary lessons taught?

Now let's take those teachers who were significant to our learning curve when we were in our teen years and early adulthood. How did we change as a result of their presence?

Who do you see as your primary teachers in these last few years? How did you meet these teachers, and what have been the most significant lessons absorbed?

Just as you've profited from teachers, who can you see as having shown up on your path seeking help? What was the most valuable tool you shared with someone else?

If you had only one tool to offer to anyone, what would it be and why? Please meditate about this idea a bit before writing your thoughts.

The Two Voices of the Mind

I spoke about this idea in other books, most recently in *Change Your Mind and Your Life Will Follow,* but perhaps you haven't read that book, so let me illustrate what I mean. It's a principle that I consider great shorthand for living our lives with remarkable simplicity. Without a doubt, I owe much of my peace of mind, my freedom from anxiety and inner turmoil, to discerning which voice is clamoring for my attention and then choosing to listen to the right one.

One of the voices in our mind represents the ego, and its sole intent is to "edge God out." Its method for accomplishing this is to speak first, speak loudly, and be committed to steering us in the wrong direction, a direction that will always run counter to the wishes or the ideas of the others sharing our path. Its primary intention is to prevent us, at all costs, from experiencing peace. The ego's purpose is to keep us uncertain and afraid and defensive, stuck and discontent.

The other voice, the one that soothes us and offers quiet, loving direction, is coming from the Holy Spirit, our "bridge" to the God of our understanding. This voice will never scream for attention, nor will it be the first to speak, but it will wait, for as long as necessary, for us to choose to hear it. The onus is on us to want to hear it, however.

Being responsible for making this choice is one of the most empowering realizations we can make in this realm of discovering who we can actually become and the impact we can have on the world around us. When we listen to this voice, we benefit and hold out hope for those who may have lost their way with our willingness to be kind, loving, and available to listen.

Perhaps the idea of having a "split mind" with two voices clamoring for your attention seems strange or unlikely to you. But ask yourself this: Has there ever been a time when you were faced with a choice and you found yourself being pulled in two diametrically opposite directions? I have, and a scenario that comes to mind right away is when I was faced with whether to go on to graduate school to complete a doctorate even though my loud ego mind was crying to be asked by my lover at the time to move with him to California.

Fortunately, he didn't ask, so I didn't really have to make the choice. I think I would have stayed behind even if he had asked. My inner spirit knew the right choice for me to make, and it would have ever so quietly convinced me. I'm almost sure of it.

Discerning the Two Voices of the Mind

The two voices are ever present. Which one we listen to makes all the difference in how we grow, how we interact with others, how we fulfill our purpose, how we add to or detract from the world around us. Discernment is the key to finding the joy that we deserve.

Are you conscious of the two voices in your mind? If you are, how would you describe them to the "uninitiated"? What would you tell them about the results you have experienced from each voice?

Because you have the power to choose the voice to which you are going to listen, are there certain steps you take to ensure you are making the right one?

When the wrong voice is allowed to direct your actions, what's the first reaction you find yourself making? Offer some examples of what you have done and how it turned out.

Shaking the Habit of Attachment

Our obsessions keep us stuck, sick, and a hostage to our own emotions as well as to the behavior of others. There is no growth for us and no benefit for our fellow travelers if this is our mind-set. Having a mind that's obsessed with others is like having no personal thoughts, or *life*, at all.

We can recognize when we have fallen prey to this way of thinking if we are honest with ourselves, but it's very difficult to shake the habit. And it is a habit! Waking up with others on our mind is second nature to the codependent. There is a "joke," that's often shared at Al-Anon meetings about the woman who, on her deathbed, in the moment right before passing, watched the lives of everyone else pass through her mind. This would be laughable if it weren't more or less true.

The value of sitting among others in groups like Al-Anon, or other spiritual support gatherings, is that we learn about another way to experience our life. And we learn this from master teachers. One of the master teachers who has impacted my life is Maggie, a woman in her eighties from Puerto Rico. Her stories are constantly illustrative of what it was like for her, what happened after becoming committed to Al-Anon, and what her life is like now. And she shares it all with humor and a wonderful, very distinct, accent.

One of the images she so eloquently shares is how Al-Anon taught her to ride in the backseat of a limousine with God as her driver. Wanting to be the driver of our own bus or limousine or truck, and everyone else's, too, is how most of us came into recovery. And even though not everyone reading this book is in recovery, I'm pretty certain we all can relate to wanting to be in control of the others sharing our path.

One of the themes of this book, and many others I have written, is how to cultivate a life that is free from the drama in the details of others' lives. Appreciating what we can learn from observing one another doesn't imply getting tangled in the web of anyone else's details. The entanglement can result in depression, or worse. Letting God be in charge of everyone is where our personal well-being and mental health rests.

I know, personally, how being obsessed with the activities of others can feel and where it can take us. Too well, I remember searching through the personal desk and dresser drawers of my lovers and even my first husband for signs of their infidelities, or driving around in the middle of the night looking for his car, certain that he was at "her" house. I don't tell you this with pride or shame, but rather honesty. I want to acknowledge who I was so that my celebration of who I am now represents the clear contrast that it is. That I changed, that I could leave the obsession and the insane behavior that resulted from it behind, means you can, too.

A point that must be stressed is that obsessive thinking is always attached to the past, generally not even something in the past that was real, or the future, about which we have no clue. When we are tuned in to *now*, that's all there is. Everything else falls away. Tuning in to now is the only trustworthy antidote to obsessive thinking. And it works.

Relief from Your Obsessions

Let's investigate your current obsessions and your progress in developing new habits and ways of thinking.

What issue or person in your life do you currently obsess over? Do you know what triggered it?

_____

_____

_____

_____

What have you learned so far from these first eight chapters that could help you find relief?

_____

_____

_____

Show how you would "activate" some of these exercises by imagining the issue or the person in a scenario in which you exhibit different behavior and thus achieve a different outcome.

Being obsessed with others, letting them have rent-free space in your mind, can be a thing of the past. You must be committed to making this change, however. No one can initiate it but you. After trying a new perspective with the most troublesome of all your "associates," maybe a colleague, a close acquaintance, or even a spouse, return here and write a brief overview of what the situation was like, what happened, and what it's like now with that person.

New habits require work, not just occasional attention. That's what this entire workbook has been about. The payoff is building, one act at a time. We aren't done yet, but we are making progress. Feel good about that. Now.

do no harm

The choice to do no harm will change your life in astounding ways.

This seems like such an obvious way to live, doesn't it? But it's not the top choice for many of us when we feel attacked or ignored or dismissed or forgotten. Life gives us lemons on a frequent basis. And just as frequently, we can make lemonade. That's the joy of understanding that what others do doesn't have to define us or our feelings or our behavior at all. We can dream about harming others, although that's never good for our soul, but we can refrain from acting on that dream. That's the good news about choices.

The ways we can harm others is as varied as the ways in which we feel harmed. Not answering when someone is speaking to you, not agreeing to discuss differences when the need is present, turning a deaf ear to the person who is deserving of a listener are all harmful acts, whether we want to admit this or not. Harm doesn't have to mean physical or even verbal abuse. Saying no words at all can harm a loved one, particularly if we are sending a message through our facial expressions. Unfortunately, we can be very creative when it comes to harming others.

We do recognize certain kinds of harm, outright, however, and the verbal kind comes quickly to mind. I grew up in a household where verbal harm was frequent. My mom was a frequent recipient of my dad's verbal abuse, as was my younger brother. My recovery eventually helped me understand what prompted this behavior in my dad, but at the time, it hurt to be a witness to it nonetheless. It wasn't that I escaped the verbal abuse, but I became steeled to it early on. I felt determined not to let him get under my skin or hurt me. Of course he did; I just never let him see it.

What I came to understand about my dad, and I think it's true regarding all others, too, is that *hurt people hurt people*. My father was a fearful man who had been hurt as a youngster. His bruises, though invisible, ran deep. His bruising of others ran deep, too. How grateful I am that I learned the value of forgiveness. It has changed how I look at all experiences in my life, those from the past and the present, too. I do not believe that healthy, whole people have any need to hurt others in any form, verbally or otherwise.

I mentioned earlier a line from *A Course in Miracles* that gives me constant strength and clarification about the circumstances I'm experiencing, but it bears repeating: "Every loving thought is true. Everything else is an appeal for healing and help, regardless of the form it takes." When others are not being kind, when others are verbally abusing us or someone else in our presence, it's their unhealthy way of appealing for help. I found this farfetched when I first read it, but it has answered so many questions for me and has brought me such peace. Now I repeat it often as a simple reminder. It's a great shorthand way of interpreting the experiences I'm having and or observing.

Be Your Best Self to Others

Let's take a look at our own behavior next. We are here to make sure our opportunities to be kind and respectful are not forsaken.

Can you think of a time recently that you didn't "show up" as your better self? Describe it and what prompted the behavior you expressed.

What's the most common way you show abuse or disrespect of others? Can you determine what's underneath your choice?

Were or are you commonly disrespected in your family of origin, or does it happen in your marriage, perhaps? If it does, what would you like to say to the "abusers" to put an end to it?

Create a brief scenario here where you are taking care of yourself in a setting that's not showing respect to you.

And now create a scenario where you are making amends by changing your behavior toward a loved one.

Deciding to Do No Harm
Requires a Daily Commitment

It's fortunate that we can begin every day all over again. Actually, we can begin every day all over again in the midst of the day itself—multiple times, in fact. The day isn't lost just because we got off the path to which we had committed. How many times have you or a friend you know given up on a diet because of a major dessert slip the day after beginning the diet? We expect perfection from ourselves, denying that we are mere humans, but for us, there is no such thing as perfection.

Being able to live only one day at a time is one of life's great gifts. Unfortunately, many of us don't accept this gift very graciously. We remain stuck in the past or "borrow" from the future and miss whatever is being sent our way on the only day we really have at our disposal. And being trapped in either the past or future is the main reason we fail, again and again, to offer our best to those with whom we are walking. *Our minds aren't here, now*, so we get edgy, fearful, and abusive in greater or lesser degrees. Fear is always at the root of our abuse. Always.

Making the decision to reframe what we are about to say, or do, could change the lives of the people we will confront every day. Our lives would reflect the change, too. We are never comforted by behavior that doesn't comfort others. *What we do to others, we do to ourselves.* That's a principle that's always true. The question is, Do we believe it, and can we use it as a guide for our actions?

Making a positive difference in the life of someone else on a daily basis would change us and them in a profound way. If you don't believe me, just try it for a week. The difference can be tiny, even unseen. Say a silent prayer, for instance. Or send flowers without claiming credit for them or maybe a loving card signed "a friend." Or be obvious about it if you'd like. That's okay, too. Just do it. Do something kind that's not expected. And don't wait for a thank-you. If you feel one is necessary, you haven't given the kindness freely. This act of kindness, for it to really count, needs to be free of all strings. Acts like these will make our default position of saying something dismissive—or worse, abusive—much less of a habit.

Bad habits aren't easy to break, but if we replace them with good habits, habits that truly feel as good to us, the giver, as they do to the receiver, our lives will change. Isn't that an appealing idea? And it's simple to execute, too. Begin by making the decision upon arising, "I will say nothing if it's not kind today."

Let's practice this for the next seven days. Keep track of how the days go. If you have a "slip," don't throw in the towel. Just think about it and take some time to write about the situation, what you did, how you felt, what you wished you had done. And if you were able to repair it, what did you do?

Day 1:

Day 2:

Day 3:

Day 4:

Day 5:

Day 6:

Day 7:

Loving Responses

This last week should have provided you with immediate feedback about the value of giving our best to others. Everyone benefits when we do. Everyone. Not just those who are in your circle of friendships but also all the men and women you will never meet. That's the power of kindness. And each of us, by refraining from doing harm, can make a profound contribution that will impact the universe for all time. Seem like a silly idea? Trust me. It's not. Truth is loving. Remember, *every loving thought is true; everything else is an appeal for healing and help, regardless of the form it takes.*

There are many simple and loving responses available to us. Recalling a few might help us remember to express one of them when we are in a situation that calls for some response. Choice is always available to us. Making the right choice is as easy as making the wrong one. And if we are still not certain of the right one, we can at least discern which one is harmless.

A few good responses to have at our fingertips at the onset of a potential argument rather than disagreeing, particularly over a matter of little importance, are smiles, affirmative nods of the head, intentional listening, perhaps saying, "Tell me more," or quietly saying, "You might be right." One of the reasons to decide not to do any harm is that we all approach situations from different perspectives. Thinking that our perspective is the only right one opens the door to a disagreement that can easily go from mild to aggressive in a matter of minutes. Nothing is to be gained by such an escalation of feelings.

Taking each of those expressions that I've suggested and practicing it would prepare you for the "real opportunity" when it comes along. Just as in the last seven days, let's take these next few days and practice, at every potential "disagreement," one of the above expressions to see how making a more peaceful, respectful choice feels.

Practicing Peaceful Responses

Day 1: If someone gets in your face or dismisses you in an unkind way, consider smiling anyway. Give this a try and share how the situation, the moment, changed for you.

Day 2: "Tell me more" is a great response and one that can diffuse a potentially volatile situation, inviting both people into a greater act of listening. Try it. Report here.

Day 3: "You might be right" is wonderfully affirming and diffusing, all at the same time. It's not a put-down of the other person. It's a way to allow both people to regroup when a discussion has gotten tense. Give this a try, and share how it felt.

Day 4: Suggesting that it's okay to agree to disagree is also a great choice when unkind words that can't be taken back are about to be uttered. This solution will save relationships of all kinds and will reap many benefits. Share your experience with it here.

Physical Harm

One form of harm we haven't addressed yet is physical harm. It happens far too often. Physical harm is less common but more dangerous than verbal abuse. The scars might not last any longer or even as long as the emotional scars of verbal abuse, but they can result in severe injury or even death. Needless to say, physical abuse is never to be tolerated. All the suggestions I have offered for handling verbal abuse don't even apply here. If you are on the receiving end of physical abuse, remove yourself immediately from the vicinity of the abuser. And if you are in a situation where you feel unable to escape, scream, kick, stomp your feet, run if at all possible, break a window or dishes, anything to attract someone's attention.

And if you are the one who has ever felt out of control, the one who was close to committing physical abuse or, in fact, did commit it, get help immediately. Most abusers have been abused themselves. Finding a solution for the rage that was no doubt triggered by fear of some kind, a rage that erupts in abuse, will take willingness, honesty, prayers, trust, time, and hope. If the abusing behavior goes unchecked, the consequences for everyone are dire, indeed. Both prisons and graveyards tell the tale.

Some of the responses that might be applicable if you are anticipating abuse are as follows:

- Leave the premises immediately.

- Turn away from the situation that is about to erupt.

- Call for help to make the right choice.

- Pray for help for yourself and the abuser.

- Pray to understand that the abuser is driven by fear, not unlike the fear you may be feeling in that moment.

- Draw up a plan for how to respond in the future if you are in the company of anyone who is bordering on violent behavior.

In the earlier days of my recovery, my husband and I drew up a "fire drill" that we would implement if either one of us relapsed. This is the kind of suggestion I'm making here. Know what you would do, have a plan, so you can best follow through. Take the time now to do this.

Plan a "Fire Drill"

My plan is as follows:

Help, Not Harm

Hurting others in any way hurts us and people on the other side of the world, too. Never doubt this. This principle is as true as "Every loving thought is true. Everything else is an appeal for healing and help, regardless of the form it takes." There simply are certain truths that must be honored. Failure to honor them adds chaos to the world around us. It's so much easier to make the choice to add benefit to the world. Choosing our thoughts and our words carefully is the easiest of all ways.

If your decision is to choose helpfulness over harm, in every instance, you will never fail to live up to the will of God. When I first came into the rooms of recovery, I drove myself crazy trying to figure out God's will for me. And then it became revealed. God's will is loving thought, in other words, kindness, quietness, prayer, the willingness to hold out hope for others, listening to someone who needs attention, offering feedback when it's requested. God's will is not complicated. It's the least complicated of all our actions.

Practicing Helpfulness	Every day provides us with opportunities to be helpful. Keep track for the next three days of what your opportunities were and how you met them.

Day 1:

Day 2:

Day 3:

Every Action Has a Wide-Sweeping Effect

Revenge is sweet, so says the poet. But is it? Whose life is bettered by revenge? The repercussions travel far and wide, and hearts are broken. Lives are shortened. Minds are poisoned. Any revenge we may think we are taking out on others is affecting us with just as much venom. *What we do to others comes back to us like a boomerang.* This is a great reminder when we are making the choice between a kind, healthy action and one that's mean-spirited.

Some of you probably remember the movie *Pay It Forward,* starring Kevin Spacey. It was about a young boy whose teacher told him and his fellow students they could make the world a better place by paying forward "the positive." I remember the movie's effect on me. The simplicity of the act of "paying it forward," when what you are paying forward is kindness and love, is mind-altering. It's capable of altering the world, too. It's a philosophy that's akin to what I'm sharing in this book. It is within our power to make a difference, now, in our lives and the lives of those who seem to be drawn to our journey.

Paying It Forward

Let's take a few minutes here and list some of the positive acts we can pay forward over the next few days. The list you come up with will be as varied as your imagination allows. The important thing is to begin looking for the opportunities to do these "random acts of kindness." Trust me when I say your self-perception will change. And how others see you will change, too.

Let's do this over the period of five days and see what the long-term effects on us are.

What can you do to make a difference?

Day 1:

Day 2:

Day 3:

Day 4:

Day 5:

What's the primary difference you can see in yourself now?

Might you consider continuing this exercise? If yes, share with someone else the value you see in this. Share those words here.

Walk Away from Arguments to Avoid Harming Others

I think it was in Al-Anon that I first heard the phrase "You don't have to join every argument you are invited to." I loved the suggestion. I felt it should be one of the primary slogans, in fact, at least for me. Prior to Al-Anon, I had never failed to join an argument that was in close proximity to me. I even joined some that weren't all that close. It was a natural reaction I developed in my family of origin where arguing was as "normal" as brushing your teeth. It wasn't that it felt good. On the contrary, arguing gave me an upset stomach, but I needed to make a point. I needed to be heard. I needed to be right. So did the person from whom I learned this: my dad.

What I have come to believe is that arguing is an attempt to cover up fear. Unfortunately, it's an attempt that has many negative consequences. And it doesn't eliminate the fear. As people respond to our argumentative stance, fear often escalates. At least that was true for me. One person finally has to be willing to step away, one argument at a time. For many years, I was incapable of being that person. Now, at last, I see the value in it.

I do want to stress, however, that we don't have to embrace the idea of giving up all arguments forever. Not when we first begin this program of change. Making the decision, one opportunity at a time, to take the high road rather than arguing is empowering in an almost indescribable way. Feeling the power of it convinced me that doing it with greater frequency made sense.

And I learned there are many ways to respond other than arguing for my position. Some of these I've mentioned in earlier sections, but they are worth mentioning again. There's making the choice to say nothing. There's making the choice to say, "You might be right." Suggesting we return to the discussion at a later time is a good one, too. My favorite is to remember that there are two kinds of business, my business and none of my business, and letting that determine my every response.

Choosing Different Responses

What I'd like to suggest to you now is to get some practice using these responses rather than arguing, regardless of how certain you are that your position is the correct one.

Share the situation and your response and how it felt to make a new response.

Opportunity 1:

Opportunity 2:

Opportunity 3:

Opportunity 4:

_____

_____

_____

How has making new choices affected you overall?

_____

_____

Would you say that you are beginning to "groove" new habits?

_____

_____

As a reminder about why we are doing this, let's recall Margaret Mead's philosophy that we change the world one person, one act, *one argument* at a time. Becoming a change agent is the real opportunity we have here.

the quiet mind

**A quiet mind knows peace,
which leads to a constant state of well-being.**

To sit alone, and in the stillness, is how we initially invite our minds to embrace the quiet. It's truly only in that stillness that we discover the peace that passes all understanding, a peace that is our birthright. This is a space I love to inhabit now. And it's a space I didn't have any experience with or access to for much of my adult life. The chatter in my mind seemed normal, and constant. I never even considered it an intrusion. A busy mind was a sign of intellect, I thought.

I don't want to suggest that thinking is bad or wasteful or that we should give it up. On the contrary, every scientist, philosopher, and writer, either dead or still alive, has relied on their ability to think through situations or experiments or creative possibilities in order to present the rest of us with their discoveries, quite often discoveries that changed the direction of the world's thinking. Consider Einstein's contributions. Or Edison's or Galileo's. Marie Curie's or Henry Ford's. We needed their willingness to live with the "busy mind." However, some would suggest that it was in their moments of stillness that their best ideas snuck in.

It's not likely that you are reading this book to create a great idea, however. More likely you are on a search for changing how your lives, and minds, currently work. And it's my contention that taking *time away,* whatever we want to call it, to let "dreams" quietly filter in is where any of us discover a new way of being. Living without perpetual angst is the dream I cultivated many years ago, and I found it was possible if I followed a few simple steps.

First, I had to allow ample time for prayer and meditation, particularly meditation. Prayer didn't really baffle me. I had made desperate attempts to talk to God for years. But I didn't know how to meditate when I began. All I knew how to do, based on others' suggestions, was sit quietly and discard, over and over, the extraneous thoughts that hounded me. The practice of sitting still, in a quiet place, even if hounded by thoughts I didn't want, was a good beginning for me, however. It was unfamiliar and gave me a sense of hope that I could attempt new activities.

Next, I invited God to come into my "empty" mind to speak words of comfort. Before long I grew very attached to those times away, whether I heard comforting words or not, and made them a daily practice, in fact. In due time, I did the practice twice daily and discovered that my state of mind, in general, was quieting. I also discovered there were many payoffs: I argued less; I worried far less. I laughed more; I lived with greater hope. But best of all, my sense of constant angst did dissipate. I had not counted on any of these outcomes, actually. The change in my state of mind was palpable. My relationships reflected the change, too. I also discovered that I didn't even have to be alone to reach this "place" of quietness. Eventually I could meditate in crowded, noisy places. The decision to go within and seek the quiet was possible anywhere. Hallelujah.

Practicing Meditation

Is meditation one of your current practices? If it is, strengthen it. If not, let me suggest you consider it now. The change you can expect in you and your relationships makes it worth the little effort it takes. Try the following:

Begin with setting aside ten minutes for quiet time immediately upon arising, right after the first cup of coffee or after reading the newspaper. Make this commitment now. Close the door to your bedroom or your office and begin, regardless of what time it is.

Report here what the experience felt like.

Was the experience pleasant enough to do again tomorrow? At least once? What specifically makes you say this?

Do this for a week and check in daily, describing how it felt and what success you had. If you do it more than once daily, make a note of that, too.

Day 1:

Day 2:

Day 3:

Day 4:

Day 5:

Day 6:

Day 7:

Is meditation making a difference in your overall experience of life? What's the overall reward you feel you are getting from meditation? Does this make it worth continuing? If not, why not?

Quieting the Mind with Meditation

Cultivating and then maintaining a peaceful, quiet mind becomes easier with practice. (I would even go so far as to say it's not possible without practice.) As I've suggested, some form of meditation will help, and there are many forms. I began with Transcendental Meditation (TM) in the mid-1970s and since then have switched to simply sitting quietly, noticing and feeling my breathing and seeing the unwanted thoughts in my mind floating quietly away.

I also practiced Walking Meditation for a period of time. Walking Meditation is a form of Buddhist meditation inspired by Thich Nhat Hanh. I continue to consider my daily walks quietly meditative. I don't try to solve problems while walking. I use the time to chat with God, as though He were an ordinary friend walking with me, seeking to know His will, all the while noticing the beauty all around me.

"Blowing away" any unnecessary thought in the midst of whatever experiences are happening is actually quite helpful. I have used this exercise thousands of times. It doesn't sound like a serious suggestion, perhaps, but because it's breaking the train of thought that has us flummoxed, or transfixed, it's surprisingly effective.

To prove my point, for this next moment, envision yourself blowing a thought away. Actually, make a relatively quiet blowing sound right now and see how this feels. Practicing this exercise along with meditation can be life changing, as strange as this may sound. You may not believe, at the moment, that this holds out much hope for success, but I can assure you, it's simple, and it works. I wouldn't suggest anything I haven't found helpful.

As you can see, there isn't any one way to cultivate the quiet mind. But there is one requirement: desire. Desire coupled with concrete willingness makes discovering the quiet place within a certainty. If sitting quietly doesn't appeal to you, that's okay. Not everyone can do it, not at first anyway. Regardless, wherever you are, finding a moment of quiet is possible, even while waiting for a green light or for the checkout line to move forward. In that moment, you will experience peace if you are open to it. In that moment, you will feel renewed and hopeful. In that moment, you will realize the closeness of God, *as you understand Him.*

Quieting the Mind

Choose any one of the mind-quieting exercises I mention above and give it some practice time now. Walk or sit or blow your troubling thoughts away. Simply be quiet.

Report here what you did and how it felt.

_____

_____

_____

_____

_____

_____

_____

_____

_____

_____

_____

Choose Your Thoughts Carefully to Feel Empowered

I used to blame others for my thoughts constantly. The blame was not just limited to how people were actually treating me but also what I imagined they were thinking of me, separate from any treatment. Blaming was so much easier than taking responsibility for anything that was happening in my life.

At that time I had no idea that assuming responsibility for what I harbored in my mind would be a good thing and would change, for the better, every experience in my life. I have mentioned innumerable times that my self-esteem was tied to *how I perceived others perceiving me.* This was never a win-win situation. And then I was introduced to another way of seeing. My life has not felt the same since then.

Being responsible for everything I think empowers me to make my life what I want it to be. Obviously this is true for you, too. For certain this doesn't give us the power to control others, nor does it prevent situations from happening that were destined to happen, but deciding how to interpret what's happening and then determining how we want to respond prevents us from feeling the sense of powerlessness that is so self-defeating.

Choosing our thoughts wisely can be turned into a very positive challenge. And when we find ourselves harboring a thought that wasn't a wise choice, we can apply one of the exercises I discuss in the previous section. For instance, close your eyes and blow the thought away, replacing it with a quiet emptiness or a fond memory of a time gone by.

Sometimes our thoughts feel too big to discard. When I struggled with the infidelities of my first husband, I didn't seem capable of discarding them. I was obsessed by his behavior. It consumed my mind. Even though it sickened me, and diminished me completely, I felt disinclined to think about anything else. Unfortunately, I hadn't been introduced to the idea of shifting my perception and asking God for the help I needed to do so.

It wasn't until I had become a student of *A Course in Miracles* a decade after the end of my first marriage that I learned how unmanageable my thinking process really was. Up until that time, whatever the proverbial "you" said or did, *real or imagined,* determined what I would say or do, as well as how I would think or feel. I had no life of my own, no thoughts separate from what I imagined yours to be, no feelings that reflected my view solely.

Gratefully, I've discovered that the only way I can "hear" and then be led by my peaceful inner voice, rather than your audible one, or even the loud ego voice in my own mind, is to be quiet enough to tune in to it. Practice and tune out those voices that may be trying to lead us away from our real purpose.

All the exercises I have outlined in this chapter have led to my being transformed and having a more manageable life and a more peaceful existence. But habit plays a huge role in how we live and think and behave. We are called upon to change our habits if we want to change our lives. I have done it, so I know you can, too. It's not rocket science. It's a spiritual exercise that begins with a little willingness.

The New You

I see it as my purpose to help you change, if that's what you want to do. Holding out hope for a fellow traveler is a great place to start the process. I have the hope for you. It's your job now to envision the person you'd rather be, the person who is quietly inner-guided, the person who is lovingly helpful to others if that's your "dream."

In the space that follows, describe who you are intent on becoming now that the invitation has been extended to you.

What do you like most about the "new you?"

Describe a scenario in which you are being this better self. What's the most obvious characteristic that has changed?

If you were going to help someone else make a change in his or her life, what would be the first suggestion you might make?

What's the most obvious impact on your relationships? Offer details here.

Cultivating a quiet mind is key to making any long-term changes in one's life. The mind that chatters all the time is exhausting. It misses the awareness of God, who is everywhere. It misses the singing birds, the breeze that blows through the trees, and the laughter of little children, along with the barking of happy dogs. It misses the thunder and the gentle rain on the roof. It misses the meowing kittens. The list is endless.

One thing is certain, however: The mind that is always speaking can't witness the others on its path. Nor can it know its own purpose, its own worth, its necessity to the journey of everyone who wanders close by. Paying homage to the quiet mind is where the kind of change we are searching for begins. Seek it now.

recognize the holy journey

**Everyone we meet is on a holy journey, just like
the one we are traveling. Embracing this idea
changes every encounter we experience,
if we let it! I know. It has happened in my life.**

This is a huge idea, and one that, if you believe it, can change every other
idea you hold. A number of years ago, *I made the decision to believe it.*
There wasn't one writer, in particular, who influenced me, or one philosopher or book or workshop or friend or spiritual teaching. When I try
to reconstruct how the change in my thinking occurred, I'd say it happened gradually as a result of the interplay of all the ideas I was being
introduced to and because I was seeking a life of greater ease, greater
simplicity, one in which I enjoyed more peace.

I was no longer interested in trying to make sense of why certain people showed up in my life and others didn't. I no longer cared why some
people were hard to tolerate and love and others felt like a blessing from
the moment we met. Embracing the idea that I was supposed to encounter all who came into my circle lessened my constant anxiety. Coming to
believe that everyone was on a "holy" mission that was connected to my
mission gave me a sense of comfort and relief.

I would have to say that this principle has answered more questions
than any other principle to which I now cling. The turmoil of my relationships in the early decades of my life, the infidelity of a former husband, the sexual abuse as a child, the acceptance and forgiveness that I

finally cultivated after growing up with a rage-filled father all had their place in the tapestry that was to become my life. I don't mean to suggest that all experiences were appreciated at the time they were occurring. On the contrary. Many were profoundly painful. Many were emotionally distressing. But with hindsight, all experiences now fit comfortably like pieces in a very large, very scenic, very intricate puzzle.

Perhaps you don't currently believe that your journey is holy and that the others whom you encounter are also traveling a holy path, but try, for now, to cast all doubt aside. Try to see those earlier, possibly troubling friendships as offering you lessons that you needed on your journey. Maybe you can see the infidelities, if there were any, as the information you can use to help others who have come to you for help. Even lessons from sexual abuse you may have suffered can be valuable for a still-suffering victim; sharing your lessons can be what he or she needs in order to realize that moving forward one day, letting go of the past, and seeing it for the lesson it offered, just as you have come to see it, is possible.

Lest I be misunderstood, I don't want to suggest that *at the moment* of any form of abuse—sexual, verbal, or physical—we can sing the praises of the experience's lessons as a holy encounter. It always requires hindsight. But healing and understanding will come. I know this. It has happened in my life, and all because I decided to believe in the "holiness" of all encounters, an idea that I will expand on in the next section.

No Experience Is Accidental

I love this idea. It cuts to the chase. It says there are *no victims,* even when we feel as if we have been victimized. This isn't easy to agree to. Without a doubt, sexual abuse feels like victimization. However, perhaps there is another way to see it. And that's what I have chosen to believe. Please hear me out. The book *Sacred Contracts*, by spiritual intuitive Caroline Myss, helped me change my idea about victimhood. She clearly states that whatever has happened in our past, is happening right now, or will happen in our future, we "agreed to" but then promptly forgot that to be the case. The "contract" was made while still "on the other side," before arriving "here" in this life experience. And the one participating in the experience with us was in full agreement with it, too.

I considered this to be a very spooky idea when I first read it. And even though I didn't initially believe it, was a bit afraid of it actually, I tried it on for size anyway. Was I in for a surprise. The transformation I felt was almost immediate. I no longer had the inner rage over the childhood sexual abuse. I was relieved of the anguish over my first husband's infidelities. I saw my father's incessant anger from a different angle. Best of all, I saw my unyielding fears, my alcoholism, and my deep-seated codependency as the tools I was to use for the growth I had agreed to experience.

In my case, and I'd guess in the case of every one of my "partners," lessons presented themselves, and I eventually learned from them. "Eventually" is the operative word here, because a lesson, if necessary to our full development, presents itself again and again in different forms until we surrender to it.

Today I can say with conviction that I hold no grudges against any of the people from my past. No one is my "hostage" today. Nor am I holding myself hostage to an old, faulty idea. And I learned the value of forgiveness, forgiveness of self as well as of others. How good it feels to have moved on. How good it feels to wake up each day knowing that what *and whom* I have sought to encounter is moving toward me. How good it feels to know that God's will for me is to say yes to each moment and every person, and that all the rest will be shown to me.

Let's take some time to explore our past, using meditation coupled with hindsight as our tools. It's an exercise that's good for the soul, and it's guaranteed to enlighten you.

Explore Your Past

What are some of your past experiences that, in a "better light," can be seen as significant lessons? Before writing, close your eyes and meditate for a few minutes. Think first of your childhood. What comes to mind first? Recall the details as clearly as possible. What do you think the underlying lesson was? How has it helped you in later years, too? Is there anything about that "lesson" that still troubles you? If so, it may well be repeated in a different form in the near future. Being troubled suggests you haven't surrendered yet.

Let's repeat the meditation exercise, letting the teenage and early adult years come to mind. What stands out as your primary struggle, and how did you resolve it? How did your resolution affect other experiences in the same time frame? If there is still resolution that's needed, how do you envision that looking?

Being alive guarantees that the "lessons" continue. That's the good news, actually. What experience have you learned the most from in the last few years? Close your eyes and let the memories fill your mind before writing.

Do you see a pattern to the lessons throughout your life? What is it?

What experience were you certain was "accidental" that hindsight has shown to be a very necessary occurrence in your development? Offer some details to clarify the necessity of it.

What "accident" has blessed you the most? List some of the ways it has enhanced the rest of your journey.

The Necessary Lesson of Every Experience

Finding the lesson in every experience lends depth, meaning, and a sense of inner joy to every waking moment. We are weaving a tapestry, one unlike anyone else's. Every experience is a thread that's needed. Looking at life from this perspective gives me great comfort and has made me realize that every event, those painful ones along with the purely whimsical ones, were necessary for my evolution. I hope you can see the value in every experience, too.

My primary lesson, as I've mentioned before, was to realize that who I was wasn't dependent on how others perceived me or treated me. My self-definition wasn't theirs to determine. Since early childhood I had lived as though everyone else was in charge of my belief system. This was not an easy pattern of belief to change. But I was helped by the idea that every action (and thought) fell into one of two categories: love or fear. When I took this to heart—and it was a system of belief that I first had to remember, then practice and finally master—my life experiences began to change. Since then, nothing has remained the same. If I'm in a situation that troubles me in any way, I ask, Is what I observe in others or feel right now representative of love or fear?

The second part of this important realization, and the part that clinches the inner change we need, is to be willing to respond in a loving way regardless of the other person's behavior. This is the acknowledgment that we *see* the experience as holy, regardless. Always, our relationships can reflect a commitment to holiness. And I've thankfully thrown my hat into *that* ring. It has made all that I see more acceptable and understandable. It has made all my decisions easier. It has clarified every experience on my radar screen, made the entrance of every person into my life make more sense, and assured me that all the yet unanswered questions can be comfortably placed on hold. The answers will come. I know.

We Meet Those Who Are Necessary for Our Unfolding

I have said this in a number of ways already, but now I want you to acknowledge it very specifically, too. In preparation, let's take some time to meditate. Breathe deeply. Open your mind to the quiet inner space that allows you to recollect who you "invited" to surface on your journey.

Throughout your childhood, every person was present quite intentionally. We don't need to focus on every one of them, but looking at a few will illustrate the point of this principle. Let's focus on your immediate family. Can you see how your interactions with them were educational, providing preparation you needed for later lessons? Envision a few of those more obvious lessons now by considering your relationships and interactions with the following:

Your mom:

How about your dad:

What did you learn from the interactions with your siblings?

Was there any friend or classmate who impacted you greatly? In what way?

Anyone else who comes to mind is important to include here in your assessment. Is there an overall pattern emerging? If so, make note of that.

We Have Chosen Our Encounters and Their Lessons

As mentioned already, my lessons were many, generally painful, and they were repeatedly reinforced. Because I didn't know who I was or my own worth, I defined myself by how others treated me, for years. I surrounded myself with people who were incapable of giving to me what they didn't have. How lovely for me that I came to believe that I specifically chose to learn these lessons, to have interactions with these very people. It has made sense of the pain and eliminated the confusion of the early decades of my life.

Because of the spiritual growth I've experienced, I can see now how perfect all those circumstances were. Our lives are divinely unfolding. Again, I repeat, we have participated in the selection process. No longer seeing myself as the victim of anything or anyone has freed me. It's a guarantee I can make to you, too. Giving up victimhood is a ticket to freedom.

Freedom from Victimhood

Claiming your freedom from victimhood can launch you forward in a new way. Meditate about the following questions and how freedom could look before responding in writing here. As practice, in the silence, create a "meeting" with a person by whom you felt victimized, and respond comfortably and with grace. Try to capture how that would feel if it really happened. Earlier in the book, I mentioned the experiment on the power of imagination with the Olympic skiing team and how I used that same visioning method in preparation for my doctoral orals. Consider doing the same here. Its power is palpable.

Is there anyone in your past by whom you felt victimized, then or now?

Would you like to take this opportunity for freedom now?

How do you see yourself now?

How do you see your interactions with the "perpetrator" after re-envisioning yourself in his or her presence?

In what additional situations do you expect to feel different? What makes you think this?

Gratitude for Encounters

It's not easy to be grateful for some of the people we encounter on our journey, at least not initially. I very recently experienced this lack of gratitude myself. Even after years of being on this spiritual path, believing in all the principles I am sharing with you, and having more than thirty-six years of recovery, I was confronted by a series of experiences with one person that unsettled me a great deal. The details aren't important. What is important to share is how easy it is to forget that God is always our comforter in every situation. I have been a steady practitioner of this idea for decades, and yet, I felt ill at ease. I found myself relieved when she didn't show up in places we both had previously frequented. I had broken one of my own significant rules: *I was giving her rent-free space in my mind.* I was letting her presence or absence contribute to how I felt.

The only way around a situation like this is to seek to see the lesson inherent in it. For me, the main lesson was to remember that, as in every other relationship or even minor encounter, we had made a "pact" on the "other side," one that was promptly forgotten. I think the lesson for me was to listen, to witness, but not to get into someone else's problem or to try to find their solution, and perhaps more important, not to be swayed by someone else's perspective. Reserve judgment always. Preserve healthy boundaries always.

Being grateful for every experience doesn't mean we have to love each experience or the person with whom we are sharing the experience. Being grateful is to accept that we will, in time, see the good in the experience. I surely wasn't grateful when my first significant boyfriend didn't want to marry me. Nor was I grateful when my first husband left me for another woman. However, the blessings I have enjoyed since surrendering to the will of God far exceed any of the good things I was sure I would miss out on if I couldn't keep my first major boyfriend and then my first husband as my hostage.

The value of making a gratitude list can't be overstated. I really didn't have much faith in a gratitude list when I first started keeping one, but I did it anyway. I had heard from so many that it significantly reframes how life looks. Indeed it does. It also is a way to thank our Higher Power for the experiences with which we are blessed. Even though many of them aren't to our liking initially, if we wait patiently, we will discover the inherent lesson of the experience.

I met a woman many years ago when I was interviewing elderly people for the book *Keepers of the Wisdom.* Alpha English was in her late eighties at the time, and she lived a phenomenal life in Menifee, Arkansas. She earned a master's degree in the mid-1930s, which was nearly unheard of for a woman at that time, particularly an African American woman. She had been a teacher and a writer of plays and books, detailing the experiences of blacks in the South. One of her plays was even performed at the Arkansas state house when Bill Clinton was governor. He honored her in a special ceremony. Being in her presence was like sitting with an angel. And her comment, repeatedly, regarding everything we talked about was "This is good." She was gratitude in action. I left her presence knowing that having and expressing gratitude for every experience was the way to guarantee a sweet life. Her life had not been easy, for sure. But she had held out for gratitude, and that made all her interactions with others a blessing to them. And she got closer to God in every instance, too. I'm sure.

Gratitude List

Let's turn to you and how you can impact your life in a positive way with a gratitude list. Write the list every night for a week, and then honestly assess how you feel at the end of the week. Each morning, perhaps over coffee, reflect on the previous day's gratitude list. It will help you be open to what comes your way each day.

At the end of each day, write a gratitude list for that day.

Night 1:

Night 2:

Night 3:

Night 4:

Night 5:

Night 6:

Night 7:

At the end of the week, how do you feel? Respond to the following questions in detail. This is for your own continuing commitment to go "to any lengths."

What's the most obvious change you detect in yourself?

How do you think others are perceiving you now?

Are your interactions and experiences with others changing? In what way?

What do you like most about your new perspective?

Has your degree of hope about the unfolding of your life, from this day forward, risen? If so, what do you most look forward to?

If there is anything else I haven't asked you to think about that you want to address, do it here:

If you don't see any difference yet, try keeping a gratitude list for another week. The point of this is to show you that your effort in seeking to see the good is what makes the good all the more apparent every day. This is your growth we are addressing, after all. And the gratitude list, like the God box exercise that is so popular among many of us in recovery, is an ongoing activity. We give our problems to God to solve when we place them in the God box, and we thank God for the good in our life when we make a gratitude list. We keep the lines of communication with God open by participating in both activities. And as Alpha would so gently say, "That is good."

The Healers on Our Path

Our relationships with others are the training ground for the lessons we are here to learn. They also provide our opportunities for a healed mind. We simply cannot heal ourselves in isolation. And we were born to be healed. As I've said innumerable times, the people on our path are here by design as the "healers" we need. They have not appeared willy-nilly. We "asked" for them, and they agreed to be part of the equation of our healing.

Now, it's true that not everyone we meet at the grocery store or everyone we pass on the street is playing a major role in our growth. But they are present, nonetheless, as opportunities for us to practice one of our major lessons: *Always express love and acceptance toward everyone.* They are opportunities for us to say, "This is good." They are opportunities for us to offer them a quiet blessing. I learned from a very good friend to say, "Bless his/her heart," every time I am feeling judgmental, whether it's toward someone I know well or someone I barely know. It's miraculous how that simple phrase changes the moment—and one's mind.

Finally, it is all about changing our mind. Changing our mind changes every experience, every relationship, every dream and hope for the future. And it reframes the past so we can see the good that was there and understand how it has contributed to the good we are experiencing now.

The Value of Each Encounter

I think looking at a few of your significant relationships, meditating on them, and writing about what you learned will help solidify the value of each encounter within them. We need to see where we were in order to see where we are now. Growth, to make it truly meaningful to us, needs reflection.

Let's begin with your most significant relationship. Close your eyes and see how it is now, as opposed to how it was. What did you specifically do to bring about the changes?

If there have been changes in your relationships with family members, write about those changes here.

How about friends and colleagues at work?

Is there someone with whom you wish there had been changes but they departed from your life before that could happen? Share what you wish, now, had been different. What, specifically, would you do differently if you had the chance?

Before moving on to the next chapter, what are you feeling most grateful for at this moment? If it relates to a person in your life, write about it here; then take the time, now, to let them know.

chapter 12

listen to the holy spirit

**There are two voices in your mind vying
for your attention. One is the ego's.
One is the Holy Spirit's. Both are patient.
Both are mind-altering. One is loud and very seductive.
We can only listen to one. Choose carefully.**

When I was introduced to this idea of the two voices a few decades ago, I wasn't sure I could relate to it let alone accept it as a premise for my life. I understood the words but not the underlying concept. Not until I began a careful review of my life and all the wrong choices I had made over the years—choices that led me sadly, sometimes dangerously, astray, choices that could have ended my life had God not intervened—did I begin to understand how easily I tuned in to the "wrong" voice. The voice that belonged to the ego. That loud, insistent voice.

I learned a lot by listening to the wrong voice, of course. I think we always do. I learned how much chaos I could create in a blink of an eye. I learned how hurtful I could be toward loved ones and strangers, too. I learned how easily I was influenced to travel down many dark alleys, trips that could have ended savagely. I learned how to sabotage my journey, again and again.

Fortunately, I gradually also learned that the pain of listening to the wrong voice was never worth the short-term pleasure it seemed to provide. This didn't prevent me from falling into its grip repeatedly anyway, but with age and maturity, I became less willing to succumb as the years passed.

I find it very interesting and valuable to reflect on the idea that I house two voices in my mind. Of course you have them, too. It means that our access to either voice is always just a decision away. My introduction to the existence of these two voices, the one that is soft and kind and loving and helpful and the one that is abusive and controlling and angry most often, came from my study of *A Course in Miracles*.

The premise of *A Course in Miracles* is to help practitioners live more peaceful lives. Its basic tenet is that we are always acting from a place of love, which is the home of the Holy Spirit, or a place of fear, which is the ego's stomping grounds. And recognizing this in ourselves and our fellow travelers makes it easier to express the love that will ease our journey and the journey of others if fear has gripped them. That's this spiritual training's appeal. Fortunately, it also complements the twelve steps, making it a perfect accompaniment to my journey.

Listen to the Right Voice

I think a valuable exercise right now is for you to reflect on some of your recent experiences, your responses, and your behavior with others that reveal the voice to which you were listening: the loving, kind voice or the loud, argumentative voice. This exercise will be enlightening. We can't change the past, but neither can we change what we don't even acknowledge. This is the first step to living differently, if that's your desire.

Take some time now to meditate first, to go within and open your mind to the experiences you have recently had. Look at them with intention. Observe what your actions, your thoughts, and your subtle manipulations were. They are the evidence of the voice to which you were listening. Don't shy away from what you see. Accepting what you see is the first step in becoming who you'd rather be.

What's an interaction you had in the past week that was a clear sign of you listening to the ego's voice?

List a few other times when you were listening to the ego's voice. Then explore, in detail, the downside each time you let the ego direct your activities and thoughts.

Listening to the softer voice of the Holy Spirit was part of your experience, too, recently. In the space below, share how it feels to listen to that voice. How do your relationships fare when it's that voice that guides your actions? Offer some instances.

Choosing the right voice takes willingness coupled with a lot of practice. There is probably at least one experience you had over the last week that could have gone better had you listened to the softer voice of the Holy Spirit. Get quiet for a moment and let it come to mind. Then describe the situation and how it could have been different.

How would your life have looked to others if you had refrained from letting the ego's voice direct you over the last month? What would have changed? Give as many examples as come to mind.

The Peaceful Voice Is the Key
to the Peaceful Journey

As I've indicated already, my commitment in life now is to be an example of and a proponent for peace, as often as possible. Getting into recovery didn't change me very much initially. As a result, I allowed the ego too much sway over my actions for too many years. But I don't want the battles anymore, and allowing the ego to rule my thoughts means battles galore. I've got the scars as evidence. However, it does take vigilance to choose again. It does take vigilance to say I want my life to look and feel different. It does take vigilance to not fall back into the old habits.

The first step is to want the peaceful journey more than the thrill of the battle. Arguing can create an adrenalin rush. And that's seductive to some. I'd have to say it appealed to me in years gone by. But listening to the softer voice, the one that seeks no adversary, the one who wants a quiet, calm heart and a sense of well-being, even in the midst of someone else's chaos, has captured me at this stage of my life.

I can't say I've always turned a deaf ear to the ego, but I have learned to say, "I need not go there." Listening to the ego has never led me into a place of solace. Listening to the ego has never benefitted me or anyone else. Listening to the ego is a clear denial of the grace that God is offering us every moment. Personally, I think we are deserving of God's grace, and I want to experience it.

Our topic here is the discovery of the avenue to peace. And it's within us every moment. It waits for our attention to it. It calls to us, but very quietly. Peace is soft and kind and comforting. Always. The voice that represents it has to also be soft and kind and comforting. It requires us to listen closely as it whispers to us. The whisper makes this voice even more appealing and inviting, I think.

Interestingly, not everyone seeks peace, and that's a fact of life. We recognize those people by their actions, their voices, their incessant attacks on others (certain popular media figures come to mind). And then there are some who would like to experience more peace, but they are afraid of the changes they will need to make in their daily responses to life. This is where we, you and I, can serve as way-showers. The changes aren't rocket science.

When I want to experience a peaceful heart in the moment, I ask myself some simple questions before responding to a situation or a person: Is what I am about to say kind and loving? Is what I am thinking at this moment of benefit to the others who are present in this sacred experience? Is what I am doing making a contribution to the well-being of the universe at large? If the answers aren't yes, each time, I need to regroup and listen more closely to the voice of the Holy Spirit within.

There are a number of other ways to achieve a more peaceful heart, too. Not joining every argument to which we are invited is an obvious one. So is choosing to see every situation and person from a different perspective if an argument or some tension is mounting. All we have to do is ask for a different perspective, and it comes calling. As I've mentioned a number of times, one way to a more peaceful heart that I find particularly appealing is to remember there are two kinds of business: my business and none of my business. Stay out of the latter! Using any one of these shortcuts guarantees more peace in the moment.

When we serve as role models for others, we are fulfilling God's will, as long as the behavior we are modeling is loving and kind. The two voices present in our minds don't deserve equal attention. The reason vigilance is so necessary though is because the louder voice is also the more insistent. Choosing to hear the quieter voice takes willingness followed by real commitment. The payoff is worth it, but honest effort is necessary.

Meditate about how you might follow a more peaceful journey before writing. Change results from your vision, your hope, and your intention.

The More Peaceful Journey

If you think you are ready for a more peaceful journey, what are some of the ways you intend to orchestrate it starting now? Journal about your vision, your hope, and your intention. Include some examples of how your everyday behavior might look if you were traveling the more peaceful journey.

I've pointed out some ways to express peace in the world that you inhabit, but I list them here again anyway for your consideration:

Smile more.

Walk away from an ugly encounter.

Say to your adversary, "You might be right."

Take a deep breath before responding to a tense situation.

Invite God into every moment.

Remind yourself that you are simply here to be "truly helpful" to the others sharing your path.

Surrender to a situation rather than attempting to control the uncontrollable.

Remember, disagreements do not require resolution.

Be kind even when others are not kind. They are simply afraid.

Perhaps you have some specific ideas, ones better than mine, for expressing peace. Remember, we can only keep that which we give away. Write your ideas here.

Be cognizant of these expressions of peace—both the ones I listed above and your own ideas—and share them with others. That's a sure way to remain committed to them yourself. Monitor your thoughts and change them if they are not loving. These are all responses that reflect attention to the voice of the Holy Spirit in our minds.

Which of these responses could you commit to immediately?

Allow yourself time to meditate about some of the recent circumstances in your life, particularly those circumstances that left you feeling ill at ease, or worse. If you had chosen your response, the experiences that grieved you would have been different. Share here your perspective on some of the experiences and the potential for utilizing the responses I've suggested.

What's the primary awareness you have gained from this exercise?

Choosing Peace

Choosing to be peaceful over needing to be right is a big challenge. But it's one you must tackle if you want your life and your relationships to change. The idea of choosing peace implies you have to give up the *need* to be "right." Giving up the *desire* to be right doesn't come as easily, perhaps, and that's okay. But in time, the choice for peace is seen to be more advantageous after all. Being soothed by this calmer choice, this quiet voice, has an appeal all its own, and this is seductive in a healthful way.

Wanting to feel better, physically, mentally, emotionally, and spiritually, is a sign that you want to grow and change and experience your real purpose in this life. That's what awaits you every time you seek to hear the voice of the Holy Spirit and allow it to make your choices, guide your actions, and direct your thoughts. I've come to believe that one of my primary purposes is to express kindness. Simple kindness. When I am being kind, in all my encounters, I feel the hand of God in my life, and that makes the moment both special and purposeful. What more could one want? For me, nothing.

Being willing to adhere to this gentle, inner voice means you will be walking away from arguments in which you need not participate. You will be allowing your adversaries to have their own opinions, and you will have no stress over your decision to keep yours as well. Healthy, peaceful relationships demand nothing less.

The interesting fact is that the more one chooses to act from a loving place, which leads always to feelings of peace, the easier the choice becomes to resist struggling with anyone over anything. I've been thinking that perhaps the desire for peace is heightened for me because of my advancing years. After all, one does get tired of tension, I think. I know I want to feel calm. I want to feel present and to serve as a loving witness to others.

Did none of this matter when I was younger? I'm honestly not sure, but the fact that I'm here in this place, now, pleases me. It has made it possible for me to stay committed to the work I do, to write books like the one you are holding, to do the speaking engagements that I love so much. And this life is all about my commitment to listening to my inner kind, gentle voice: listening to its words of comfort, to its suggestions to express only love, to its song of forgiveness. Your life, and mine, too, and thus all our relationships, can't be anything but mellow when we turn our minds, *and our behavior,* over to the power of the loving voice that's always waiting for our willing attention.

Taking an inventory of your relationships periodically is an enlightening experience. I think the time for doing so is now.

I suggest you find a quiet place to rest awhile. Turn off your phone and the light if that helps. Close the door and the shades, too, if you so choose. Now sit down in a comfortable chair,

Inventory Your Relationships

breathe deeply, and allow the many relationships that you are presently in travel through your mind. Notice them, one by one. Notice, explicitly, your behavior. Which relationships create tension in you? See if you can discern why. And notice the ones that make you smile. Now just sit quietly with your recollections.

After twenty or thirty minutes of silent reflection, begin writing about your observations. What you write is for your eyes only, unless you want to share it. This exercise is meant to open your eyes to who you most commonly are.

What did you notice about your behavior in your most significant relationship? Were you proud of it?

Did you notice any difference in your behavior with friends as opposed to the most "significant" relationship partner? Explore those differences here and see if you can discern why the difference exists.

What do your interactions generally look like with strangers? Is there anything about that behavior you'd like to change? What do you think the payoff might be if you behaved differently?

After making these observations, can you think of at least three changes you would like to make in your behavior, with both friends and strangers? List those changes here.

Consider, before moving on, if you were to always put your best foot forward, how would you present yourself in every encounter? Describe yourself here. Your recent reflecting will help you with this exercise. Offer some specific imaginary encounters with detailed habits you can fall back on when you do have the chance to put that best foot forward. You will discover many of them.

Old Perspectives Control Old Behaviors

Old perspectives are generally tied to the ego's voice, the voice that has held sway too often. Old perspectives die a slow death. What I am suggesting here is that we be willing to discard those old perspectives, which means turning a deaf ear to the ego and allowing the Holy Spirit's voice to guide the changes that would benefit our behavior and thus all our relationships, too. Think of this as an adventure. A game, perhaps. Practice watching yourself as you go through a day, noticing how many times you put your best foot forward.

It is practice that molds us into the people we'd rather be. There is no mystery here. You can make any change you really want to make. Start small, however. Try applying Mother Teresa's principle for living: *Be kind to everyone, and start with the person standing next to you.*

Practicing New Principles of Living

Let's delve deeper into these suggestions. Share what you wish in regard to these questions before we move along.

If you were to take just one suggestion that I've made, or the one from Mother Teresa, and apply it for one week, how would your life look? How would you feel? How might your relationships change?

Now practice Mother Teresa's suggestion for a week. Very honestly, share how your interactions seemed to change.

What did you learn from doing this?

Is it a suggestion that you find worthy of practicing daily? Why?

The Timeline Is Yours

There is no timeline for changing ourselves. There is no requirement that we change at all, in fact. But it's my guess that most of you who have stuck with this book want to make changes, or you would have put the book aside a long time ago. I'm delighted you stayed with the process. There is so much we can do singly and collectively to make life better, for ourselves and others, too. But the first requirement is willingness. The second is to stay committed, even when you want to quit.

For every person any one of us touches with our kinder, gentler behavior, I have heard it said that seven more are touched, too. Paying it forward is one way of describing it. The impact each of us can have on the world around us by simply treating every person we encounter with kindness is almost beyond belief. In fact, I think that's the calling with which each of us has been blessed. Many of us have simply been unaware of it. Until now. Listening to the softer, ever-present voice in your mind prepares you to fulfill that calling; it's one that graces every experience you will ever have.

New Behaviors

I invite you to list those new behaviors you plan to adopt from this day forward. I invite you to make a contract with a friend that you will meet or call to check in with, on a regular basis, regarding the behaviors you are committed to changing. Perhaps you and your friend can form a support group that includes others who want to live better, more peaceful lives, too. Helping one another along the path to greater peace is how the world around us changes.

List the new behaviors you plan to adopt here:

Joy awaits you. I promise. Agitation can be over. I promise. Arguments can be over. I promise. Tension can be gone. This I promise, too. Applying the suggestions I lay out in this book guarantees that relationships can be calm and peaceful and loving. The time to begin changing is up to you. This book and its suggestions will always be within reach. Go forth and have fun. A better life is waiting for you.

summary and quick review exercises

A lot has been covered in this small workbook. But like I have said throughout, we can start our process for change in a small way by taking one suggestion at a time and applying it for a day or even an hour and then observing how different we feel, how different our relationships feel, and how even one small change seems to affect the behavior of the many people we are encountering, whether they are friends or complete strangers.

We can't pick up a book like this and assume that one quick read of it will work a miracle, that every relationship will immediately improve. We can assume, however, that the application of a tiny suggestion, repeatedly practiced, will guarantee a miraculous result. Eventually. Let's not forget that *nothing changes, if nothing changes*.

To make it easier, I've listed here all the suggestions I've made throughout the book to reiterate the lessons and exercises you've already encountered. However, I do advise you to reread the book in a few months and do the exercises again, at least part of them, just in case you need a tune-up. Most of us do need tune-ups occasionally. That's certainly been my history.

Chapter 1: Let Go

**If we don't give others their freedom,
we will have no freedom either.**

- Notice who you are trying to control.

- Let others live without your interference.

- Who would/could you be if you weren't trying to control others?

- Live in your own hula hoop, and give others the freedom to do likewise.

- Letting go means taking no hostages and embracing your freedom.

- How does a life without hostages look?

Before moving on to the next chapter's overview, let's evaluate your progress:

How well are you doing with letting go? Share a few comments here:

Is there a pattern to your "stuckness" with this principle? If so, what it is?

What solution makes sense? After applying it for a week or two, share how that has worked.

_____

_____

Chapter 2: Getting Unstuck

Put your attention where it belongs:
On yourself. On your life.

- Shifting your perception is an obvious way to get unstuck.

- Shifting your perception can release you from the problem altogether.

- We can learn how to let go of unhelpful feelings and thoughts, with practice.

- Feelings are not facts.

- We often overreact based on erroneous assumptions. This never has to happen again.

- Making more productive, thoughtful choices is possible if we are willing.

- One of the smartest choices might be *to do nothing*.

- Remember, the behavior of others never requires a response.

- A basic premise for cultivating the quiet life is to avoid getting into business that is not yours.

- Disengage from chaos, wherever it is found.

- Detach from the behavior of others. Never let it define you or control you.

- Use the principle "I can see peace instead of this" often.

- Say a prayer for others, friends and strangers alike.

- Walk away when the world around you is getting "noisy."

- No one's bait need ever hook us. We are not fish.

- Relax. Enjoy the moment. That's all there is.

Before moving on, let's check in on your progress:

Is there one of these suggestions and/or principles that has worked extremely well for you already? If so, share your experience with it here before going on.

Is there one that has you baffled and troubled? Write about it here. Sometimes revisiting it will give you a new insight.

Chapter 3: Let Go of Outcomes

Because we are members of the human community, letting go is a constant in our lives.

Being surrounded by friends and strangers at every turn forces us to be vigilant in our commitment to living one life only—our own. But this chapter is focused only on outcomes.

Remember, God is in charge of outcomes, which limits the "job" we need to do. Outcomes are not our purview. Effort is our work, and our only work.

- Obviously, God is also in charge of all people, relieving us of that duty, too.

- Our "work" is attending to *our* affairs, *our* business, and *our* lives, including the tiniest of details. Of course, God is available to us in every instance.

- Appreciating the present, really absorbing its every detail, keeps your focus off of the future, everyone's future.

- Joy is only discovered *here, now.* Seek it completely.

Before moving on to the next chapter's overview, let's measure our progress.

After reading this chapter earlier and doing the exercises that were included, how do you rate your progress with letting go of outcomes? Please be honest with yourself. That's how real growth occurs. Share your progress here.

What do you see as the area that needs the most attention?

Chapter 4: Changing Our Minds

We can expect miraculous results when we focus on shifting our self-perceptions along with our perceptions of myriad situations, people, places, and things.

Changing our minds in regard to every person, place, situation, and experience is life-altering for sure.

- How we see a person is based on a choice we have made. If we want to see the person differently, we have to be willing to let go of our drama about them.

- Every time we become willing to see a person, whether a friend or a stranger, differently, we are demonstrating our willingness to grow into a more peaceful person.

- There is great personal power to be attained when we apply this tool. No person remains the same to us when we have committed to seeing him in his best light. And that's the payoff for both of us.

- To attain peace of mind, which, in the final analysis, is the focus of this book, we must be willing to change any thought that isn't contributing to a feeling of peace. Vigilance and willingness are the necessary ingredients.

- Use of the imagination, as detailed in the story about the Olympic trials, is a powerful tool. It will change your self-perception. It will change your ability to succeed. It will reduce, even possibly eliminate entirely, your fear. It did eliminate mine.

Let's evaluate ourselves for a brief spell here.

How successful have you been at changing your mind in those situations that called for it?

Have you met with success in any of your relationship struggles when you focused on simply changing your mind?

Did you try imagining yourself in full control of your reactions within a particular situation? How did it feel?

Did you use this tool when dealing with a fear-filled situation? What was your experience with it? Did the fear leave you?

Chapter 5: Choose Your Reactions

**Knowing how and when to detach
is the tool we need to hone.**

Knowing the difference between acting and reacting, and letting our knowledge guide us, promises a far different set of life experiences.

- Avoiding knee-jerk reactions will save us from many unnecessary conflicts and the accompanying emotional inner turmoil.

- If we recognize whose business is whose, we will more willingly attend only to our own. This takes intense honesty. And fortitude. And daily willingness.

- The recognition that others' mood swings are theirs and in no way related to us will serve as the catalyst for our self-direction and our freedom. It also frees us from guilt, shame, and the fear of incompetence that have troubled so many of us.

Let's do an exercise or two before moving on.

What was your most recent overreaction? Describe it in detail. What did it accomplish—or not?

Mood swings can seem very powerful. How did you maintain equilibrium during your most recent experience with someone's vile behavior or mood swing?

Can you detect a changing mood in yourself? What do you do to temper it?

Chapter 6: Give Up Negative Judgments

**Every loving thought is true. Everything else
is an appeal for healing and help,
regardless of the form it takes.**

We must give up negative judgments, all of them. They cannot serve us, or our universe, in a loving way. Remember the following always:

- Our companions are our teachers.

- You and I must be willing to change if we want changed, peaceful relationships.

- What we do to one, we do to all.

- We must be willing to shift our perceptions if we want to be free of fear. Here are two helpful hints to do this:

  - Remember, you and I are here by divine appointment.

  - Our companions are our *appointed* and intentional learning partners.

- We can choose peace over being right by using the following simple suggestions:

  - Say nothing.

  - Leave the room.

  - Agree with your adversary by saying, "You could be right." This simple statement diffuses any and all situations.

  - Make a gratitude list before bedtime.

  - Appreciate each encounter.

- We are being sent the people we need in order to grow and to make our finest contributions.

Let's evaluate your progress:

You have had time to appreciate the value of your many companions on this path. What's the most important thing you have learned from applying a few of these suggestions for choosing peace?

Write about your most changed relationship. Are you experiencing greater peace? What's the one thing that stands out most in your mind about the changes that have occurred?

If you were to give someone else only one piece of advice based on your experience, what would it be?

Chapter 7: Accept the Gift of Powerlessness

**If we want peaceful lives,
we must engage in peaceful behavior.**

We are powerless over others, and that's a gift. However, it takes time and willingness to appreciate the depth of this gift, the gift of real life for us.

- Give up trying to control others. It's a burden and will never lead to peace.

- Let others go, one by one.

- Remember, we are not powerless over ourselves, our own responsibilities, or our own willingness (or not) to forgive.

- Shifting our perceptions about others is the key to moving on.

- Let everything fall away but your dependence on God.

- Follow your own path; it's divinely yours. The same is true for everyone else you meet.

- Give all people, all decisions, all solutions to God.

Before moving on, let's check in with how you've been applying these techniques.

What's the most peaceful behavior in which you have recently engaged, with whom, and what were the results?

If you were to make a suggestion to a friend so she might try to experience more peace, what would it be?

Chapter 8: Discover Your Own Lessons

**Our relationships are our training ground
for every lesson to which we will be introduced
in this life. Looking at them closely, surrendering
to the lessons, and appreciating the "giver"
of each lesson makes the journey we share holy.**

Our relationships will benefit if we remember the following:

- Our journey with others can be a minefield.

- We can too easily overstep the boundaries between us.

- The dance of codependency is addictive.

- Our primary lesson is to control only ourselves.

- Our vigilance must be constant.

- The ego cries to get us involved in the business of others.

- Detachment is a loving gift we can give to everyone in every relationship we have.

- Emotional maturity relies on us practicing the following ideas:

  - Every loving thought is true; everything else is a call for help.

  - We meet everyone we need to meet.

- You need never be held hostage by someone else's behavior.

- Be the loving witness your companions deserve.

- Practice kindness in every encounter.

- You have one life to live. Live it well.

- We are present to each other to serve each other.

- We are on assignment. Do your work!

- Refrain from giving your mind over to someone else's story—their past, present, and future.

- Our obsession with others prevents us from knowing ourselves. Our calling here is to know ourselves and do that which is God's will.

Before moving on, let's pause to re-explore this chapter's lessons.

How would you assess your progress on the points outlined for this chapter? Share here what has worked well for you.

Share what still needs vigilant attention. And remember, practice is what's required. Perfection is unattainable, and that's okay with God.

Chapter 9: Do No Harm

Hurt people hurt people.

This popular axiom explains a great deal when we consider the many injustices that occur every day. I think this explanation can apply to all affairs, perhaps worldwide.

Let's review how we can forge a new way to experience the people and the situations we encounter. There are myriad ways, and they are all simple and easily performed.

- Be kind, regardless of how the other person is behaving.

- Make a daily commitment to look at each person you meet and smile at them.

- Remember, what we do to others, we do to ourselves.

- If what you are about to say isn't loving, reframe it so it is.

- Make a positive difference in someone's life every day, with no strings attached.

- Make a promise to yourself, and God, every day that you will say nothing that isn't loving and kind and helpful.

- Always give your best to others.

- Remember the following easy solutions that will change you and your relationships: smile, listen, nod lovingly when listening to someone speaking to you, say, "You might be right," when having a disagreement, say to an adversary, "Tell me more."

- If physical harm is about to happen, do none of the above. Leave the premises. Don't do anything to escalate it. Never initiate it.

- Hurting anyone hurts everyone.

- Every action anyone takes affects others like the ripples in a lake.

- Every morning and in every situation, ask, What can I do to make a positive difference?

- Take the high road if conflict is imminent.

Take a moment to reflect on this chapter's lessons and exercises.

How would you rate yourself on these many suggestions? On what are you basing your rating?

Which of these suggestions has become second nature to you?

How different are you feeling now in all your relationships? Which suggestion has made the greatest impact on your most significant relationships?

Chapter 10: The Quiet Mind

**Cultivating a quiet mind is exceedingly beneficial
to us as individuals and to our companions,
and thus the whole universe, too.**

There are many ways to cultivate a quiet mind:

- Practice daily prayer of any form.

- Practice daily meditation, such as sitting or walking meditation.

- Intentionally appreciate nature.

- Light a candle and watch the flame.

- Listen to quiet music.

- Imagine God, and let all else fall away.

The importance of cultivating the quiet mind is the understanding that we are empowered, *or not,* by the thoughts we are thinking. The above methods are just a few ways of achieving it. The quiet prepares us for changing them.

When thoughts come in, during meditation, invite them to leave. Even blow them away. They will go. If voices come in during meditation, listen only to the most quiet one. Choose wisely. Peace relies on your choice.

Let's evaluate how we are doing with these techniques.

Are you finding a specific time to pray every day? If so, what is the major gift it has given you?

Meditation is often harder than prayer. Have you been successful? If so, which form of meditation has worked best for you?

Are you seeing the connection between having a quieter mind and living in more peaceful relationships? Share what this has been like so you can come back to it in those times when you have forgotten and gone off track. That will happen.

Chapter 11: Recognize the Holy Journey

**If we recognize that we are all
intentionally sharing this one holy path,
it makes it easier to see one another as worthy.**

Being able to change how we perceive every person, every situation, everything is truly a miracle.

The first time I heard that a "miracle" was a simple shift in perception, my radar went up. I both wanted to experience the miracle and doubted the validity of the statement. Indeed it was and is true. Nothing in my experience has stayed the same since that time. And now you have had time to experiment, too, with shifting your perception.

Our decision to see others as essential to the holiness of our individual journey is the key step that must precede all others.

- Be willing to change how we see everyone.

- The shift in perception will astonish us.

- It's not as hard as it first sounds.

- Asking the God of your understanding guarantees that the shift in perception will occur.

Let's review your success.

What has been the best payoff from asking God to help you see a situation differently?

If you didn't get the results you had hoped for, ask again and again. We are not striving for perfection. We are seeking joy. Let's review some of the additional principles from this chapter:

- We are like pieces of a very intricate puzzle. Every one of us is necessary to the completed picture.

- We have all *volunteered* for the our part of the picture. We are not victims.

- No experience we had along the way was accidental. Every experience lent vibrancy to the evolving picture.

- Learning to give up hostage taking, so everyone could fulfill his own assignments on this journey, was the best gift of all we can give to ourselves.

- We are always in the teaching/learning mode. And that is good.

- Giving up grudges and not taking hostages lightens the load in our minds.

- Respond with love, regardless of the experience.

- Every encounter is a holy encounter.

- Our relationships are the training ground for the peaceful life that we seek.

- Respond to every occurrence with "This is good," and all else will fall away.

Before moving on to the review of the final chapter, let's recall some of the key experiences we've had and discern what they taught us.

Looking back, what can you say now was the most enlightening experience you had while doing the exercises in this book?

When you think of your life as part of an intricate puzzle, what aspects please you the most?

How do you interpret "holy" in terms of the following thought: We are making a holy journey and every encounter we have with any one is a holy encounter.

What has most changed for you since reframing your life in terms of seeing it as holy?

What have you learned that you most want to share with others?

Chapter 12: Listen to the Holy Spirit

Two voices are vying for our attention,
but we can only listen to one at a time.

This particular principle, if applied with our best interests in mind, would change all our relationships in a nanosecond.

Let's focus on the specific things we need to remember so we will choose the right voice to hear:

- Wrong choices are very easy to make.

- The ego is one of the voices that's always present, and it's loud, insistent, and offers wrong advice.

- The Holy Spirit is just as present, but its voice is gentle and kind. Not pushy. And we have to lean into it to hear it.

- Vigilance regarding our choice is mandatory.

- Remember, peace is our goal.

- Ask yourself if others will benefit from your thoughts and actions.

- We can walk away rather than argue. This is often an excellent choice.

- Discerning what is your business and what is none of your business can be best addressed if you choose to listen to the "right voice."

- You are choosing to be peaceful rather than to be right. Never forget that, and your journey will be smooth.

- The loving Holy Spirit is always waiting to lead us to the place of a peaceful heart.

- Making the decision to put your best foot forward could create the dream life you long for.

- Every principle in this book is easy to apply. However, practice is as necessary to changing your life as brushing your teeth is to avoiding cavities.

Let's measure our progress for now. It is my hope that you will want to continue making progress in the months ahead.

On a scale of 1 to 10, how peaceful is your life? Offer some evidence of things that have happened that revealed your level of peace.

On a scale of 1 to 10, how peaceful are your relationships?

What voice seems to dominate, and how does that manifest on a daily basis?

What's the most beneficial thing you have done for others since reading this book and practicing these exercises?

Would you agree that you are living up to God's expectations of you with greater ease than before? What is the most current example of that?

epilogue

In closing, I want to thank you all for joining me on this journey. Not just this journey through the book, but also this journey through life. Even though we haven't touched one another, flesh to flesh, we have touched one another. I feel your presence in my life every day. And it creates a level of joy in me for which I can't even find words.

I wish it were possible to meet each of you in person, but we will visit, *on the other side*. Of that I have grown quite certain.

May peace be your constant companion.

about the author

Karen Casey is the author of twenty-six books, many of which have been translated into more than a dozen languages. Her own recovery from alcoholism along with her commitment to helping others heal themselves have made her a much sought-after speaker at recovery and spirituality conferences throughout the country. She and her husband divide their time between Florida, Indiana, and Minnesota.

Visit her website at *www.womens-spirituality.com* to read her blog. Find her on Facebook (Karen Casey and friends) and follow her on Twitter (@Caseykaren) too.